D1592585

منقوشة Man'oushé

Inside the Lebanese Street Corner Bakery

Barbara Abdeni Massaad

Photography by Barbara Abdeni Massaad and Raymond Yazbeck

Interlink Books

In loving memory
of Amer Ishak
1990–2008

To the young man who always delivered *mana'ish* to our neighborhood with a warm smile. He was accidentally run over by a car working on a delivery. May you rest in peace, Amer; we miss you.

First American edition published in 2014 by

INTERLINK BOOKS
An imprint of Interlink Publishing Group, Inc.
46 Crosby Street
Northampton, Massachusetts 01060
www.interlinkbooks.com

Text and photos copyright © Barbara Abdeni Massaad, 2014
Photos pages 4, 7 right (top & bottom), 20, 22 upper left, 23, 25, 26, 27, 30 (upper left), 42, 43, 46, 56, 66, 67, 73, 74, 90, 93, 106, 108 (upper left), 139, 149 (upper right), 155, 156, 159, 163, 171, 191, 194 © Raymond Yazbeck, 2014
Photos pages 19 (left), 77, 152 © Serge Massaad, 2014
Illustration page 15 © Albert Serge Massaad, 2014
Drawings page 13 © Tabary Editions (reproduced with kind permission)

Library of Congress Cataloging-in-Publication Data
Massaad, Barbara Abdeni.
Man'oushé : inside the Lebanese street corner bakery / Barbara Abdeni Massaad ; photography by Barbara Abdeni Massaad and Raymond Yazbeck. – First American edition.
    pages cm
Includes index.
ISBN 978-1-56656-928-6
1. Cooking, Lebanese. I. Title.
TX725.L4M38 2014
641.595692–dc23
                                    2013032109

General Editor: Michel S. Moushabeck
Editor: Leyla Moushabeck
Copyeditor: Kitty Florey
Proofreader: Jennifer M. Staltare
Cover design: Julian Ramirez
Book layout and design: Mirna Hamady

Printed and bound in China

To request our complete 48-page, full-color catalog, please call us toll free at 1-800-238-LINK, visit our website: www.interlinkbooks.com, or send us an e-mail: info@interlinkbooks.com

If you bake bread with indifference, you bake a bitter bread that feeds but half of man's hunger.

Gibran Khalil Gibran

Contents

المحتويات

Introduction	7
Life's Journey	11
Ingredients & Cooking Tools	29
The Basics	41
Wild Thyme	53
Cheese	69
Dried Yogurt and Bulgar	93
Turnovers	105
Vegetarian	113
Egg	125
Chicken	131
Meat Preserve	137
Meat	149
Ground Meat, Onion, and Parsley	167
Armenian Sausage	177
Sweet	183
Index	198

Introduction

The *man'oushé* is the quintessential Lebanese breakfast. Named for the Arabic word *na'sh*, which refers to the way the fingertips of the baker "engrave" the dough, the *man'oushé* is indeed engraved upon our collective memories as Lebanese. The smell of *man'oushé bi-za'tar* in the morning catapults a Lebanese person back in time to a lively childhood birthday party, breakfast on the go with classmates before an exam, or a cozy morning spent tête-à-tête with a loved one.

Satisfying and tasty, it is truly a classless commodity. Tiny bakeries across the country sell this disc of dough pressed flat and baked with a topping of wild thyme, sumac, sesame seeds, salt, and oil. One can find a *man'oushé* literally anywhere, from the poorest neighborhoods to the most affluent of Beirut's suburbs. Inexpensive and delicious, it is one of Lebanon's common denominators.

Forn Saydaleh in Baabda opened its doors 150 years ago. Mr. Kanaan Saydaleh, the owner, operates this bakery with his wife, as he has done for over half a century. Mrs. Saydaleh kindly peeled a fresh orange for me as we sat down to discuss the history of the *forn*, the Lebanese street corner bakery.

In past generations, no one purchased bread. Bread dough was made at home daily and taken to the village *forn* (meaning oven) to be baked for a small fee. The expression *niswan al-forn* refers to the ladies who sat and talked while they waited for their bread to bake. Today, the term is used to describe women who love to gossip. The baker has an important task in the community, as shown in the proverb: "*A 'ti khubzak li-l-khubbaz wa law akal nusso*," meaning: "Give your bread to a baker, even if he eats half of it."

▲ A mural layout of a street corner bakery in the back roads of Saida.

▲ Mr. and Mrs. Saydaleh; hospitality the Lebanese way.

◄ Fingertips of the baker "engraving" the dough.

▲ These wooden panels are typically used in all bakeries to hold flat discs of dough before they enter the oven.

▲ A villager from Hrajel in the Kesserouan area. He and his wife operate a small, cozy bakery.

With the automation of bread-making, these small bakeries ceased to bake bread for customers, offering *mana'ish* (plural for *man'oushé*) instead. From wild thyme bread, *mana'ish* became a word used to describe a wide array of pies baked at the *forn*, topped with cheese, meat, or vegetables—even sweet pies.

It seems every customer has a favorite way to eat the *man'oushé*. I have so often witnessed men who bluster into the bakery and order: "*Sabaho! Buddi man'oushé 'ala zaw'ak!*" which literally means "Good morning! I want a *man'oushé* made to your liking!" This places the baker in a position of trust. Women tend to be more particular about how their *man'oushé* is prepared, often to the extent of bringing in their own toppings and asking the baker to work under their supervision.

The bakery has always been a meeting place. People sit down together to discuss politics and current events. Newspapers are read from cover to cover and passed on to the next table. Ladies enter in groups to enjoy a *subhiyeh* (a morning meeting). Once I witnessed a blossoming romance between the baker and a young woman ordering a cheese pie. Her intentions were so obvious that the baker winked at me as he prepared her order with extra care.

There is a certain satisfaction to be found in preparing your own *man'oushé*. The recipes included in this book are the result of thorough research of traditional recipes from across the country, mixed with a twist of personal creativity. It is up to you to put the two together. By all means, experiment with these recipes and add your personal touch. You will taste the difference!

This book represents tiny pieces of a puzzle that make up moments of my life and the stepping-stone of a unique journey, a journey I would like to share with you.

▶ It is typical for a woman to bring her homemade *za'tar* mixture to the nearest street corner bakery.

Life's Journey

I vividly remember the details of my arrival in Lebanon. The smell was the first thing that struck me. The air was stuffy and condensed, different from what I had been used to. I was terrified by the sounds at the port of Beirut. In the late 1980s arrival in Lebanon on a boat from Larnaca was an adventure that lasted two days. Hearing the Arabic language for the first time seemed strange to me, especially as I heard it being shouted. Lebanese people don't talk, they shout. I have become one of them.

I remember the way up the mountains filled with broken-down buildings, broken-down roads, and what looked like to me broken-down people. It was a day in mid-February in the year 1988, just a few months before I was due to graduate from Cardinal Gibbon High School, the dream of any American child.

Our house stood in the mountains of the Kesserouan, an hour drive from the capital. It felt cold and damp, a world away from sunny Florida. It was odd to come back to the place that had haunted me for so many years. This was the house I had lived in as a young child, a house full of fond memories of a girl picking all the wild daisies in the garden, riding her bicycle, playing with her dog, pretending to sail the high seas in a broken boat at the end of the yard.

The first thing I did upon entering the house was to open the refrigerator. This gives you an idea of where my priorities lay! Inside I found an assortment of local cheeses. There was a bag of Arabic bread on the counter. The keeper had made this gesture to welcome us. I suppose the message got through because, to this day, I remember this specific sign of hospitality—an important characteristic of Lebanese people. It certainly helped me to adapt and embrace my new life here.

I was ten years old when we immigrated to the United States. I fell comfortably into the system and over the years studied like any other American kid. I can still remember when my 5th grade teacher, Mrs. Eden, asked me to make a Lebanese dish for my classmates. My mother made the traditional *tabbouleh* and I felt very proud that day walking into the classroom wearing her *'abayaa*—a traditional Lebanese dress.

The years passed. I became an American. An incident in high school during religion class brought the memories and nostalgia I had buried deep inside jarringly back to the surface. The class was discussing current events. The professor mentioned Beirut, Lebanon. A student stood up and said arrogantly, "Why don't they just blow up Beirut to solve the whole Middle East problem!" I was devastated. I realized then that I was not immune to my origins.

I often dreamed of being in Lebanon, only to wake up in the States. The comfortable sense of living in Lebanon, as in one big village, faded with life in the States, with its huge population and its large cities.

▲ Our family restaurant
in Florida, USA.

The Family Restaurant

When I was fifteen, my life changed considerably the day my father, a professional photographer, decided to go into the restaurant business. I vaguely remember him purchasing and painting doors and gathering odds and ends from the house to decorate the restaurant. I worked with him for hours on a blue and gray arabesque mosaic. And then one day, Kebabs & Things opened its doors. It was a family business in the real sense of the word. My father was in charge of the restaurant, my mother handled the accounting matters very diligently, and my sister and I helped in the kitchen and served the customers. Haygas, the chef, a man of Armenian origins, would explain patiently how to make the food and drop in a few words about Tina Turner's legs.

My father photographed a mouthwatering platter of Lebanese appetizers to entice customers at the entrance. My mother, sister, and I were in charge of seating customers. Communicating with your elders at an early age can be quite intimidating. Regardless, when confronted with such a situation, you make the best of it. Every night, practice made perfect; after a while, it became second nature.

In one instance, the food we served in the restaurant seemed to make a group of Middle Eastern men very happy. They were loud, hungry, and visibly enjoying themselves. They asked me if I could play a tape for them. The music was wonderful. As a gesture of friendship, they let us keep it. *Linda, Linda, ya Linda… layliyi as-sahara inda…,* a popular Lebanese song, became an important aspect of the restaurant's ambiance. I can still remember teaching my friends to belly dance to this tune, barely knowing myself how to move.

The restaurant years were not always easy, but were part of growing up. I sometimes wondered why I couldn't be like everyone else. I still recall a long walk home the day I had decided to leave the restaurant business. My father had hired a homeless Lebanese man to help us do the dishes. I was angry because I had to share my tips with this man. I was so upset that I told my father, "I quit!" and stormed out of the restaurant. The walk

Lunch ★ Dinner ★

RESTAURANT

2768 East Oakland Park Blvd.
(East Oakland Park & Bayview)

Goscinny–Tabary © Tabary Editions–2009

▲ Armand, a friend of
my father's playing his
guitar for our farewell
party.

home was long, but fruitful, because it made me realize how selfish I was. As soon as I reached home, I called my father and asked him if he wanted me to come back, to which he answered, "Rest today, you will come back tomorrow night."

On Valentine's Day, I told my father, "Debbie's parents invited me to have dinner in a fancy restaurant, and I have accepted. You'll have to do without me tonight!" I really wanted to go out to a nice restaurant, to be waited on for once instead of waiting on others. Before leaving, I called to confirm that all was going well. My father told me that it was quiet and that he probably would close early. Relieved, I left with a clear conscience. Debbie's parents treated us to an unforgettable evening. While I was having a wonderful time, my father, mother, and sister struggled through the busiest night that the restaurant had ever known. People lingered outside waiting for a table. Everyone was in love and hungry.

For quite a while, my father toyed with the idea of returning to Lebanon. I guess a Lebanese person never feels whole anywhere else but in his country. I can understand this now, but at the time my parents' decision to leave the United States bewildered me.

▲ George and Laurence
Abdeni, my parents,
in 1987.

We sold the restaurant to a Spanish man who transformed Kebabs & Things into a Spanish cantina. But can the soul of a restaurant be erased with a mere change of decor?

I shall never forget the going-away party held at the restaurant. All our close friends gathered with tasty Lebanese food, nostalgic songs, and dance. For me, it was not a celebration, but one more memory to cherish before we left. The day of our departure had finally arrived. My sister and I cried like we had never cried before. I remember Anna Christina, my mother's friend telling me "Don't leave, stay; if you want to stay, stay!" It was impossible. We were already leaving for the airport now, and nothing could stop us. I saw my friends fading as the car drove away. Their lives continued. Mine was shattered.

Motherhood

My life, which had seemed to be on hold, took a new start when I met Serge. I was eighteen years old, full of dreams and desperation.

I remember myself as an eight-year-old, on the school bus, dreaming of a blond boy with curly hair. I married that boy seventeen years later. Serge helped me transfer my diploma so I could continue my studies and enter university.

A couple of months later, war struck again in Lebanon, leaving us confused. Maybe I had to live through a part of the war in order to become a real Lebanese.

A few years later, Serge and I were married in Byblos, at St. John-Marc, a beautiful Roman style church built at the beginning of the thirteenth century. For our honeymoon, the obvious destination was the United States. Returning to America was an experience I needed to start my new life, without looking back.

Pregnancy came as a total surprise to us. Ironically, that same week, I had been offered the job of a lifetime. The only condition that the company set for my employment package was that I not get pregnant for the first two years of employment. Needless to say, I didn't take the job.

To this day, I believe that motherhood is my greatest achievement ever. Our son Albert's birth triggered our family to grow fast. In a matter of four years, Albert, Maria, and Sarah were born. Being of a possessive nature, thus wanting to do everything myself, the task I had set for myself was quite demanding and tiresome. The kitchen provided me with an escape. Over time my focus became dough-making. I find that making dough is very gratifying. Not only is kneading the dough therapeutic, the process is also so much more than simply mixing ingredients together. Dough is a living organism that needs time to rest before it becomes edible. It needs nurturing and care. The end result proves it.

I often joke with my children, telling them that the dough has to sleep before we can play with it, or cook it. Their show of interest encourages me to teach them more.

◄ Wild daisies always remind me of my carefree youth.

▼ My son Albert's perception of his parents' role: "Papi is making money, Mami is making pizza."

Apprenticeship

When my third child, Sarah, started preschool, my mornings were suddenly free. Naturally I asked myself, "What am I going to do with the rest of my days?" Nostalgic thoughts of the restaurant came to mind.

One day, it hit me. I was going back to learning. What would be the one thing that could be useful to me both as a homemaker and as a building block to a future career? Cooking! This was the perfect moment for me to start my culinary journey. After much thought, I decided that the best schooling I could get would be to train in a restaurant.

A friend introduced me to the owners of a French restaurant, who agreed to let me come in every morning for the kitchen preparations. Not only was French cuisine a new venture for me, but I also knew it was the foundation of culinary education.

The kitchen became my second home, my haven. Everything made sense. After a while, business slowed down and I had learned what I could. Then, luckily, I was introduced to a man who owns a chain of reputable restaurants in Beirut. He let me start training in an Italian restaurant due to close in two months.

On the first day of my training, the manager tried to warn me about the strange character of the head of the kitchen, Chef Franco. This made me a little nervous, but nothing was going to get in my way of learning the tricks to making delicious Italian cuisine.

Chef Franco turned out to be a warm, affectionate, and, above all, professional chef. His gift to me was the passing on of his special pizza sauce recipe. I promised never to tell a soul.

My next culinary venture was in a reputable Lebanese restaurant. Entering a new kitchen in a restaurant is like dipping your toes in water to test the temperature before jumping into a pool. What I experienced in this kitchen was a true revelation. I discovered that Lebanon holds a very interesting array of people with different backgrounds. Lebanese food is one of the best cuisines in the world, and all this was here for me to discover. I only had to go out and reach for it.

I studied every aspect of this new kitchen. I enjoyed myself and wrote down every single detail of my training. Everyone participated in giving me extensive explanations.

The spot in the kitchen I enjoyed most was the baker's corner. Every morning, Mohammed made mounds of dough to bake Lebanese bread. The bread emerged from the oven steaming hot and smelling delicious. He explained to me in detail how to prepare the dough and make small balls that were left to rise in floured wooden boxes carefully stacked high. Here is where I had the idea to conduct a thorough research of the *man'oushé*.

All too soon, my training was over. I sought the advice of the manager who had shown me around the Italian restaurant, hoping he could draw a career path for me. His answer was sarcastic and almost offensive: "Putting on a chef's uniform does not make you one!" I stayed home feeling sorry for myself, but it only lasted a week.

Main à la Pâte

As the saying goes, "A long journey starts with one single step." The first thing I did was to visit the bakery across the street from my house, in the suburbs of Beirut. I introduced myself to the owner and told him about my quest. He agreed to help me, and thus my training started inside the *forn*. I had already acquired some experience from my training in the Lebanese restaurant, and my pizza-making skills were also very useful. But here it was different. I was actually making *mana'ish*, and slowly but surely learning how to prepare all the delicious pies served in the Lebanese bakery.

It was very exciting because I felt like I had my own bakery. I served customers, put the prepared pies into the hot oven, made balls of dough from a big pile of flour in the dough mixer, or simply watched the scene from afar. I wore a white apron with a white bonnet, something I learned from my restaurant training. It attracted curiosity. Customers would enter, take a look at me and wink at the baker, intrigued. A full discussion of my mission ensued—curiosity being another distinctive Lebanese trait.

The baker showed me the steps to make the different pies. First I learned to make big mounds of dough in the dough mixer. Bakers always say, "The dough can play tricks on you. You have to be very careful to monitor the weather conditions and act accordingly. This comes with experience." Next I learned to operate a machine called the *rekaka*. Timing your moves can be tricky; as one piece of dough comes out, another has to be inserted immediately. You must be skilled because the machine runs very quickly. One false move and the dough is knocked off and falls flat on the ground. It is lots of fun. When my son learned to operate the *rekaka* one Saturday morning, he was covered with flour from head to toe.

▼ Making flat discs with one's hands takes practice and skill.

Spreading the toppings evenly across the dough also takes practice. Too much or too little of the topping makes a big difference. I found that the best way to spread the toppings on the different pies is with your hands. Quite elementary, but very efficient!

Finally, sliding the pies from the wooden board into the gas-fired oven requires real skill and a quick little snap of the wrist. I practiced doing it with a mocking baker over my shoulder. Not an easy task!

An important aspect of my research was to visually document my journey. Photography was a crucial part of my childhood. I remember my parents waking me up in the middle of the night when I was four years old. My mother would put makeup on me, and my father would take beautiful portraits that I still cherish. When I was fifteen, my father gave me one of his cameras, and I would photograph everything and anything.

When I first started researching *man'oushé*, I was convinced that I needed a professional photographer. My father did not agree and encouraged me to take the pictures myself.

My husband's cousin, Nabih, introduced me to Ray, a renowned professional photographer. On our first meeting, I told him about my project, seeking to involve him. He was hesitant, for he was working on his own books. He was also very busy with other professional commitments. It seemed a lost cause. I paid him a visit the next day to further discuss my idea. I guess I was convincing, because he agreed to try a session with me on the following week. He took beautiful pictures, which have become part of my documentation, and then he encouraged me to take my own. I was reluctant at first. Later, nothing could stop me. It became almost an addiction, a passion encoded in my genes.

The team was set. I did my research while he worked on his books. In the process, he taught me a lot about photography.

We visited every corner of Lebanon. We had endless conversations with hundreds of people. At midday, he would always get hungry and insist on tasting the *hommos bi-tahini* of the given region we were visiting. After such a meal, I would get sleepy; contrarily, he would be ready to start over again.

On April 23, 2004, my father gave me all his camera equipment. It was very symbolic, like a message for me to carry on his task. I was very happy, and at the same time it was heartbreaking.

The Places

On a cold winter day, we set forth on our first photo excursion. "We must go to Baalbek today! I want to take a picture of Baalbek in the snow," suggested Ray. It had snowed heavily in the mountains that night, and Ray did not want to waste an opportunity for that specific photograph. I was reluctant, fearing the slippery roads of Dahr al-Baidar. But then again, I pictured the ancient Roman city wrapped in a blanket of snow, and the venture suddenly seemed quite appealing!

Exploring my native country, from north to south, allowed me to embrace it wholeheartedly. With each trip, my roots grew deeper and stronger. The places I have visited bring forth special memories of picturesque landmarks, beautiful natural landscapes, cities, towns, and villages filled with contrasting scenery.

Lebanon is not one culture or scene. It is a multitude of sights, sounds, and smells that flash in my mind: the congested streets of Beirut, where modern and ancient cultures rub shoulders, the ancient crowded markets of Tripoli and their mystical narrow alleyways that take you back in time. It is the unending sight of the blue Mediterranean Sea, where fishermen ply their age-old trade. It is the peaceful fields of the Beqa' Valley, where peasants, dressed in colorful attire, pick the fruits of their hard labor. It is the infant perched on his father's shoulders, proudly carrying a decorated candle to celebrate Palm Sunday outside a remote village church. It is the muezzin's cry at sunset, on top of Mount 'Akroum in 'Akkar, calling Muslim worshippers to prayer. It is the traditional *mezze* served in small pottery dishes on the riverbanks of al-Berdawni in Zahleh. It is the Cedars of Lebanon surviving nature's devastation. It is all this, and so much more…

▼ In the souk of Saida, this man takes a break to smoke his *nargileh*.

▼ These men play backgammon in the Shouf on a daily basis.

◄ Baalbek, the famous ancient Roman temple, in the snow.

Life's Journey | 21

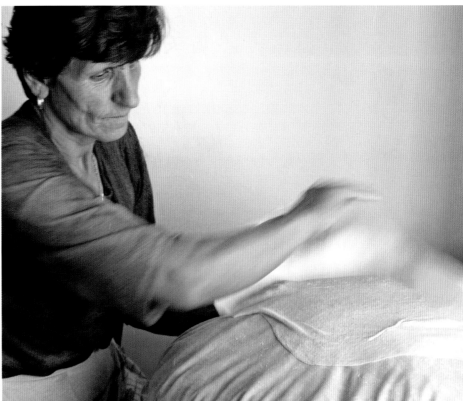

The People

As extraordinary a place as Lebanon is, my journey became truly unforgettable mostly because of the human aspect. I learned the ways of the Lebanese people: their generosity towards strangers, their appetite for conversation, their need to share life stories, and their love of food. It was a joy to be among them.

On the same street, three shops down from the first bakery where my training started, stands a small bakery owned by a man called Fares. I entered his bakery with the same scenario that I would present to each baker. He was friendly and answered all my questions. I asked him why he became a baker. He smiled. "This answer needs time." I retorted, "I've got all the time you need!"

It was raining outside, and customers were scarce. Fares and I sat down in his bakery for three consecutive hours. As the story of his life unfolded before me, tears ran down my cheeks.

Fares was born in Bayno 'Akkar, in the extreme north of Lebanon. He comes from a poor family and is the youngest of eleven children. According to him, his mother had time and affection for only three. Fares's father was a farmer, working odd jobs that could not give his family financial stability. Life was hard. Fares's childhood memories are not happy ones. He quit school early. A family dispute led him to Beirut. At the age of eight, Fares found himself alone and scared at nightfall under a bridge. A woman in a nearby building offered him refuge for the night and helped him find a job in a factory.

This job didn't last. Fares found work in a bread bakery. The owner asked him, "What can you do, son?" Fares replied, "Anything at all!" This is where he learned the ropes to become a baker.

The young boy became a man. With his savings, he took on the responsibility of opening his own bakery. He worked very hard, yet was fulfilled by his success.

▲ Ghalayini Bakery in Hamra.

▲ Mrs. Boyagian making metallic convex discs in her small workshop in Sed al Baushrieh.

Another person with determination and strength, whom I met when I visited different bakeries in Lebanon, is Mrs. Coharik Ichkhanian. Her face inspires trust and wisdom. I met Mrs. Ichkhanian at her bakery on an early morning and asked her to talk to me about her famous Armenian meat pies. The discussion took another turn, and, before I knew it, we were discussing memories of a lifetime.

"I am the youngest of five children. My parents were Armenians living in Syria. I did not finish my schooling because, at the time, it was not considered appropriate for a woman to be educated. My husband and I met through relatives and married in Beirut in 1975, just after the war began." In 1984, Coharik's husband died at the age of 44, leaving her with three young children. She started working at the bakery in 1985. Business was at its best during the war. The bakery was full of customers. People had to eat. "Food was a therapy for all." In the neighborhood, she has become the food expert, the reference. Coharik personally goes to the market to handpick the ingredients for her distinctive meat pies. She explains that they have a unique taste; unchanged since the bakery opened. When I asked her why she didn't make any other kind of pies, she answered: "The other recipes are not Armenian!" Coharik generously shared her life stories and her precious recipes with me.

In Lebanon, the best and the most common way to find a specific location is to ask people on the road for directions. Needless to say, their advice is not always accurate, but it will give you an idea of where you should be heading. I stopped once to ask a woman for directions. She was carrying a handful of fruits. She showed me the way and spilled all the fruits into the car, offering them to me as a gesture of friendship and hospitality.

Mr. Lahoud, a jovial elderly man intrigued by my interrogation at his cousin's bakery, unraveled his philosophies of life with romantic poems and anecdotes, all spoken in Arabic. The one sentence that I was able to fully understand was, "Live your life as if this was your last hour." I looked at him approvingly. Then, out of the blue, he asked me for a kiss. I was surprised, yet I thought, "What the heck, if it makes his day, why not!" We burst out laughing.

The journey I underwent to accomplish the task I set out to do has helped me to grow as a person. It is a door that has been wide open for all to see. It is the discovery of a national culinary tradition, simplified and explained for all to discover. It is a unique portrayal built within the roots of a small country in the Middle East, my country, Lebanon.

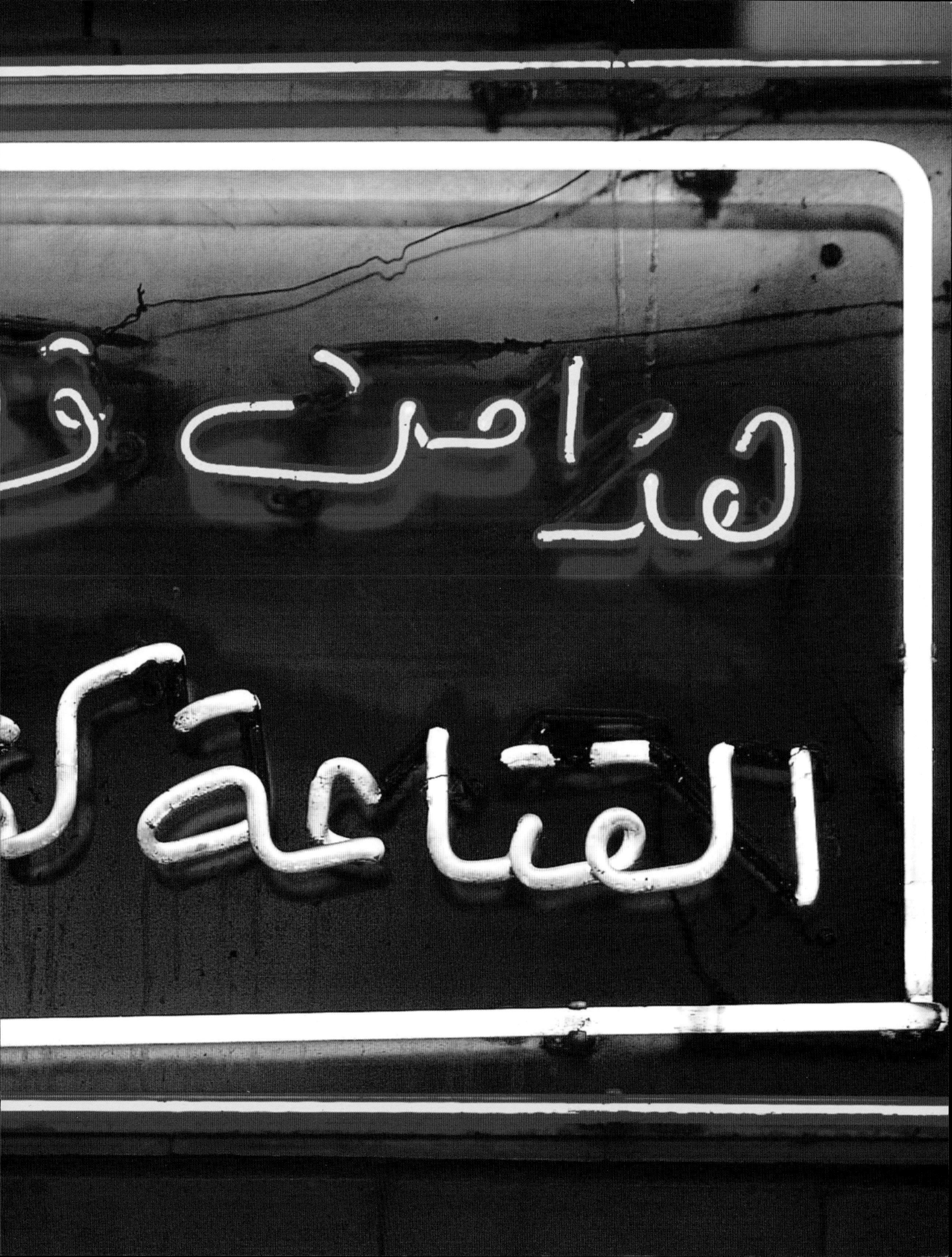

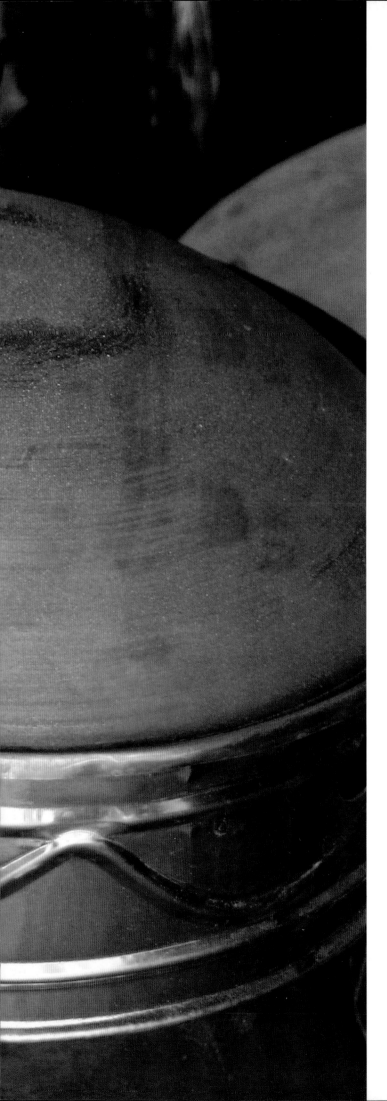

المكونات وأدوات المطبخ

Ingredients & Cooking Tools

Ingredients

Kitchen Tools

Cooking Methods

Ingredients

Wild thyme mixture (*khaltet al-za'tar*)

Lebanese thyme mixture (*za'tar*)
A mixture of dried wild thyme, sumac, sesame seeds, and salt (see recipe on page 54).

Aleppo thyme mixture (*za'tar halabi*)
A wild thyme mixture typical of Aleppo, Syria. It often contains ground pistachio, ground chickpeas, and sometimes aniseed, among other ingredients.

Orange blossom water (*ma' zahr*)

Fragrant water distilled from macerated flowers of the Seville orange (*bou sfeir*).

Paste (*ribb*)

Hot red pepper paste (*ribb al-harr*)
Imperative for lovers of spicy food (see recipe on page 153).

Tomato paste (*ribb al-banadura*)
Use of store-bought tomato paste is acceptable, but nothing beats homemade tomato paste.

Pomegranate syrup (*ribb al-rumman*)

Thick syrup made by boiling the juice of sour pomegranates until it is reduced to a thick, dark-brown syrup. Sometimes also called pomegranate molasses.

Molasses (*debs*)

Thick dark syrup extracted from carob pods or made by reducing aging grapes.

Wheat (*qamh*)

Bulgar / cracked wheat (*burghul*)
Boiled, dried, and partially debranned cracked wheat. It is available in different textures, from fine to coarse. You will need fine bulgar for the recipes in this book.

Kishk
Bulgar (cracked wheat) fermented with yogurt. After fermentation it is salted, spread on a cloth to dry, then finely ground and stored for use (see recipe on p. 97).

Flour (*tahin*)

White bread / strong flour (*tahin zero*)
This high-gluten flour makes a crisp, chewy, firm crust.

Cake flour (*tahin extra*)
This type of flour gives the crust a softer texture.

Whole-wheat / whole-grain flour (*tahin baladi / tahin asmar*)
Flour made from the whole grains of wheat. In Lebanon, it is often ground and used immediately. It is the best flour for making paper-thin bread (*khobz marquq*, p. 48).

Cornmeal (*tahin dura*)
Coarse, yellow-colored flour made from ground corn kernels. It can be sprinkled on the work surface before rolling to give the dough texture.

Semolina (*smeed*)
A granular flour made from wheat middlings, a by-product of processing wheat into flour. You will need durum semolina, which is yellow and made from hard wheat (soft-wheat semolina is white).

Yeast (*khamireh*)

Starter (*tarbayeh*)
The traditional method used to leaven the dough for bread-making. This method is still practiced in villages, especially when making paper-thin bread (*khobz marquq*, p. 48). There is no need to dilute a yeast starter.

Baker's or fresh yeast
If available, it is a good choice. It is sold in blocks and must be diluted in water. It can be stored in the freezer for up to six months.

Active dry yeast
For best results every time.

Fast acting yeast
Useful if you are in a hurry, but certainly not recommended.

Phyllo pastry (*'ajineh r'i'a*)

Paper-thin sheets of pastry dough, used for flaky sweet or savory pastries. It can found in supermarkets, fresh or frozen.

Dairy (*ajbân wa albân*)

'Akkawi cheese (*'akkawi*)
A salty, semi-hard white cheese made from cow's milk. It has a fibrous, rubbery texture. It is stored in salted water and is the most suitable cheese for the cheese pie. Substitute firm mozzarella if you can't find it.

Bulgari / Bulgarian cheese (*Bulghari*)
A sharp, white, sheep's-milk cheese resembling feta but with a stronger taste. It is usually sold in blocks. Substitute Greek feta.

Halloumi cheese (*halloum*)
A salty, semi-hard cheese made from sheep's or cow's milk. It has a fibrous, rubbery texture and is often used in cooking.

Kashkaval cheese (*ash'awan*)
Yellowish cheese with a tangy flavor encased in a rind. It can be made of sheep's milk or cow's milk. It is similar to pecorino Toscano.

Feta cheese (*feta*)
A pure white, brined curd cheese characterized by its crumbly texture and high salt content.

Whey cheese (*arisheh*)
A curdled whey cheese resembling cottage cheese. In the process of making *'akkawi* cheese, the whey is cooked with additional milk and citric acid. It coagulates and curdles, thus creating its unique consistency. Substitute ricotta.

Spiced cheese balls (*shankleesh*)
Cheese made of curdled whey, which has been drained and hung to dry. It is then mixed with a blend of spices, dried in the sun, and stored in airtight containers to ferment. The cheese balls are then washed and rolled in dried thyme (*za'tar*) or other herbs (see recipe on p. 77).

Yogurt (*laban*)
A custard-like food made from cow's, sheep's, or goat's milk. It is produced by bacterial fermentation of milk.

Strained yogurt (*labneh*)
Yogurt strained through cheesecloth until it is the consistency of cream cheese (see recipe on p. 85).

Meat (*lahmeh*)

Meat preserve (*awarma*)
Lamb preserved in fat. It is known as the villager's winter meat preserve (see recipe on page 138).

Beef (*lahmeh baqar*)
Look for good-quality lean meat with a small quantity of fat for extra flavor.

Lamb (*lahmeh ghanam*)
The first choice for meat pies. Look for good-quality meat.

Armenian sausages (*sujuk*)
A spicy air-dried lamb or beef sausage, usually flavored with cumin, allspice, cinnamon, garlic, and red chili pepper flakes.

Spices (*bharat*)

Cumin (*kammun*)
The dried seed of the herb *Cuminum cyminum*, a member of the parsley family. It is a pungent and bitter-tasting spice.

Allspice (*bhar helo*)
A flavorful spice widely used in Lebanese cuisine.

Red pepper powder (*bhar ahmar*)
A spice made of dried hot and sweet red peppers.

Seven spice (*sab' bharat*)
A Lebanese spice mixture containing black pepper, white pepper, allspice, cinnamon, cloves, nutmeg, and coriander.

Sumac (*suma'*)
Astringent, dark-red berries of a Mediterranean shrub, dried and ground into a powder. Sumac has a pleasant sour taste. It is sometimes used as a substitute for lemon.

Aniseed (*yansun*)
A sweet-smelling, strong-flavored spice, often used in sweets or infused to make a popular hot drink called *yansun*.

Mahlab (*mahlab*)
A spice made from pits of sour cherries and often used to flavor sweets. You can substitute ground apricot kernels or fennel.

Nigella seeds (*habbet al-barakeh*)
Small black seeds with a peppery taste, typically sprinkled on breads and cakes. Not to be confused with black sesame seeds.

Sesame (*sumsum*)

Sesame seeds (*sumsum*)
Pale cream-colored seeds of a plant widely grown in tropical regions. They are oily and highly nutritious.

Sesame paste (*tahini*)
Thick paste made from ground sesame seeds.

Halawa (*haleweh*)
A bittersweet dessert in the form of a hard paste made of the roots of the halva plant mixed with sesame paste (*tahini*).

Oil (*zeit*)

Olive oil (*zeit zeitoun*)
Use good-quality extra virgin olive oil.

Vegetable oil (*zeit nabaati*)
Any good-quality vegetable oil will do.

Kitchen Tools

Baker's peel

This is a flat paddle used to slide pies in and out of the oven. Dust it with flour before using to keep the dough from sticking.

Baking or pizza stone

Baking dough directly on a baking stone helps to evenly distribute the heat for a crisper crust and a more authentic flavor. Baking stones are useful for making sure your Arabic bread (*khobz 'Arabi*, p. 45) puffs up. If you don't have one, you can use unglazed clay tiles, a crisping pan (my preference), or an upturned baking tray. Make sure to place your baking stone in the oven before preheating, and allow it to cool gradually, or it can crack.

Cheesecloth

This muslin cloth is used in the making of *labneh*, *shankleesh*, and *kishk*. Alternatively, you can use a clean white pillowcase that has been washed with natural soap.

Cheese grater

This is used in some recipes to grate cheese or vegetables.

Colander

This is important for draining the ingredients that would otherwise make your pies too soggy.

Dough scraper

This can help you cut dough evenly and manipulate sticky pieces.

Flour sifter

It is necessary to sift some flours to achieve a more homogeneous texture in your dough.

Food processor or stand mixer

The dough can be made in less than five minutes in a food processor or stand mixer. You will also need a food processor to make the toppings for several pies.

Hand-woven baskets

When baking bread on a convex metal disc (*saj*), these traditional Lebanese woven baskets are used to receive and cool finished pies. They are typically large enough to fit the paper-thin bread (*khobz marquq*, p. 48).

Heavy-bottomed casserole

This is needed to prepare the cooked toppings and fillings.

Kitchen scale

Use a digital scale for precise measurements.

Jars

Jars are used to store red pepper paste (*ribb al-haar*, p. 153) and meat preserve (*awarma*, p. 138).

Measuring cups and spoons

These are a basic necessity in any kitchen.

Mortar and pestle

This is useful for grinding whole spices or crushing garlic (along with fine salt) to obtain the smooth paste needed for some recipes.

Pastry brush

This will help you coat your turnovers evenly with a light layer of oil for crisper dough.

Rolling pin

You will need two rolling pins. Use a long, lightweight rolling pin for very thin dough. Use a shorter and heavier rolling pin for thicker pies.

Circular cushion (*kara*)

This firm cushion is traditionally used in the making of paper-thin bread (*khobz marquq*, p. 48) or clay-oven (*tannur*) bread. The dough is stretched evenly across it before it is flipped onto the hot surface of the convex metal disc (*saj*) or clay oven. Unfortunately, it is not easy to find a traditional *kara*. If you sew, you can make one yourself, using tightly-woven cheesecloth or muslin. Stuff it with regular batting and make sure it is the same size as your heat source.

Wooden table (*tablieh*)

Before baking, the dough is traditionally flattened on small table, placed next to the convex metal disc (*saj*).

Spatula

If you are using a convex metal disc (*saj*) or cast-iron griddle, keep a few metal spatulas on hand to manipulate the pies. They keep your fingers away from the burning heat of the cooking surface.

Spray bottle

Use for misting the surface of the convex metal disc (*saj*) or cast-iron griddle between pies. This prevents the dough from sticking and debris from gathering.

White sheet (*mizar*) or dish towel

This is used to cover the dough while it slowly rises. It should be damp during use.

Cooking Methods

Conventional oven

All the recipes included in this book have been tested in a conventional oven. For best results, it is imperative to preheat the oven for at least 15 to 20 minutes before baking the pies. It is also important to place your pies in the hottest part of your oven. Baking your bread directly on a baking stone or a baking tray also helps. I use holed crisping pans and get very good results every time.

Convex metal disc

The traditional way to cook these recipes is on a convex metal disc (*saj*). In the past, the convex disc was set on stones, and dry branches were burned under the disc to heat it from below. Today, most use an apparatus where a gas burner can control the intensity of the heat. If you have access to a *saj*, I highly recommend it, not only for added flavor, but for the ritual itself. The first time may be a bit difficult, but with practice it becomes quite simple.

Griddle

My mother once gave me heavy cast-iron griddle pan. She bakes her bread on the griddle on the stovetop as an alternative to using a convex disc (*saj*). She had hers made by a skilled craftsman. I use it all the time. You can use any large, flat cast-iron skillet, griddle, or crepe pan.

Cook's Tip: The convex disc and the griddle need to be preheated before use. This will disinfect the surface and make crisper dough. Spray with water when surface is hot and in between pies. The water will evaporate immediately. Don't ever wash the convex disc or the griddle with heavy soap and water. When not in use, coat the surface with a pastry brush dipped in vegetable oil to prevent rusting.

Baker's oven

In Lebanon, it is common to make one's topping mixture and take it to the neighborhood bakery to have the baker bake it in his / her oven. The baker spreads the mixture onto the prepared dough, lays the pies on wooden baker's peels, and bakes them in the scorching-hot oven. The baker's oven is special because it preserves the heat inside. It has a very hot stone floor; thus the pie cooks quickly and evenly. The scorching air causes the dough to form bubbles, a typical characteristic of the *man'oushé*. In the past, burning wood or fuel oil was used to feed the fire. Today, flames are ignited on both sides of the oven by gas fuel.

Clay oven

The clay oven (*tannur*) is another traditional way of baking bread. It is built in a hole in the ground in the form of a large barrel. The inner sides of the barrel are lined with clay. The core of the oven is left unpolished. It is heated with dry wooden branches. In the past, baking bread in the clay oven was a collective activity done among women of the village. The dough is stuck on the inner sides of the clay oven with the help of a cushion (*kara*). One minute later, deliciously scented bread comes out steaming with flavor. Today, baking in a clay oven is a rarity, but a tradition very much appreciated.

▶ Baking bread in a
tannur, an ancient
tradition, in a bakery in
the souk of Baalbek.

The Basics

أساسيات الخبز

The Dough

Arabic Bread

Paper-Thin Bread

The Dough

Al-'ajeen

This technique will teach you how to make the dough with no fuss. For a heartier, robust flavor, you can replace the bread (strong) flour with whole-wheat (whole-grain) flour. You can also substitute all-purpose (plain) flour, but your dough will have a different texture.

2½ cups (13oz / 360g) of white bread (strong) flour

1 cup (5oz / 150g) of cake flour

1 teaspoon of active dry yeast

1¼ cups (300ml) of lukewarm water (body temperature is best)

2 teaspoons of salt

1 tablespoon of sugar

1 tablespoon of vegetable oil

1. Measure the flours.

2. Dissolve the yeast in the water and set aside for a couple of minutes. Sift flour and salt together into a bowl and stir in the sugar (it is important to mix the dry ingredients first).

3. Gradually pour the yeast water and the oil into the dry ingredients and mix.

4. Knead the mixture to make soft dough.

5. Tip the dough onto a lightly floured surface and knead for 5 to 10 minutes until smooth and elastic. (If you are using a food processor or stand mixer, add the dry ingredients first, then gradually add the liquids. Start at a low speed, and gradually turn up the speed, running the machine for 1 minute. Always stand close to the machine while it is running.)

6. Place the dough in a large bowl dusted with extra flour or greased with olive oil (this will prevent the dough from sticking to the surface of the bowl). Cover the bowl with a damp dish towel and leave to rise in a warm place, free of drafts, for 1½ to 2 hours, or until doubled in bulk. I usually place my dough in an unheated oven to rise.

7. Punch down the dough. On a floured surface, form the dough into a log. Pinch off the dough to form 4 equal-sized balls (unless otherwise specified in the pie recipe). Flour or grease the bowl again and leave to rise for an additional half-hour.

8. Flatten each ball with your palm.

9. Using a rolling pin, roll out each ball of dough into a disc of about 10in (25cm) and a thickness of ¼in (6mm).

10. If you are using a conventional oven, spread the circles onto a baking or crisping pan or place your baking stone (see p. 35) on the bottom shelf of the oven before preheating.

 Yields 4 pies.

▶ Fresh loaves of Arabic
bread carried by a boy
in the souk of Tripoli.

Arabic Bread

Arabic pita bread (*khobz 'Arabi*) is flat, circular two-layered bread that is usually about 10 inches (25cm) in diameter. It is split to make a sandwich, or broken apart to be used as a utensil for scooping foods. Pieces of this bread are used to clean the last bits of stew from one's plate. It can be eaten alongside everything from dips and appetizers to everyday meals. This bread is distinguished by the hollow pocket that forms during baking. The bread puffs roundly in the hot oven, and falls as it cools. The flavor of the bread is best when it is fresh and hot from the oven. Its fragrance is unforgettable!

In the past, women in Lebanon used to make their own bread at home. A woman kneeling in front of a large copper basin, kneading her dough and pounding it with her fist, was a typical sight. The dough was often taken to the local bakery (*forn*) to be cooked in the hot oven. The dough would be carried home, hot and fragrant, on a large wooden or straw tray made by Lebanese artisans.

Today, Arabic bread is most commonly bought fresh from local bakeries. Bakeries have become a big industry in Lebanon, catering to every kind of customer. Today, the procedure of commercial bread-making is done with sophisticated machinery that fills up whole rooms. I visited a large bakery in Beirut and found it fascinating. The owner explained the several stages to me: mixing the dough, breaking it apart into balls, flattening it, leavening it, and letting the dough rest before baking it in the hot oven. Finally, it is put neatly into plastic bags and sent to the storefront to be sold. It is quite impressive.

But the feeling you get when you bake your own bread is unbeatable! The first time I made Arabic bread, I felt so proud to invite my family to eat these delicious loaves. Initially, it may seem difficult, but with practice you will find yourself making bread easily and often. The secret to successfully baking Arabic bread is to preheat your oven very well; 15 to 20 minutes should be sufficient for the bread to puff and make the hollow pocket in the middle. If you can, use a baking stone.

Arabic Bread

Khobz 'Arabi

خبز عربي

1 teaspoon of active dry yeast

1¼ cups (300ml) of lukewarm water (body temperature is best)

2½ cups (13oz / 360g) of white bread (strong) flour

1 cup (5oz / 150g) of cake flour

1 teaspoon of salt

1 teaspoon of sugar

1 tablespoon of olive oil

1. Dissolve the yeast in the water and set aside for a couple of minutes. Sift flours and salt together into a bowl and stir in the sugar. It is important to mix the dry ingredients first.

2. Stir the oil into the yeast water and pour into a large bowl.

3. Gradually beat the flour into the yeast mixture, and then knead the mixture to make a soft dough.

4. Tip the dough on to a lightly floured surface and knead for 5 to 10 minutes until smooth and elastic. (If you are using a food processor or stand mixer, run the machine for 1 minute. Start at a low speed, then gradually turn up the speed. Always stand close to the machine while it is running.)

5. Place the dough in a large bowl dusted with extra flour or greased with olive oil. Cover the bowl with a damp dish towel and leave to rise in a warm place free of drafts for 1½ to 2 hours, or until doubled in bulk. I usually place my dough in an unheated oven to rise.

6. Punch down the dough. On a floured surface, form the dough into a log. Pinch off the dough to form 6 to 8 equal pieces, depending on how thin you like your bread.

7. Place a baking stone or upturned baking tray on the bottom shelf of your oven and preheat to 425°F (220°C / Gas mark 7).

8. Using a rolling pin, roll out each ball of dough into a circle of about 10in (25cm). Cover again and set aside for 10 minutes.

9. Place the circles directly on the baking tray or stone and bake for 3 to 5 minutes, watching carefully so they don't burn. Your bread is ready when a hollow pocket has formed and the bread is slightly browned on the edges and on the top.

10. Arabic bread is best eaten hot out of the oven because it tends to dry out quickly. If you want to store the bread for later consumption, allow the bread to cool, flatten, then store in sealed plastic bags in the refrigerator or freezer.

 Yields 6 to 8 loaves.

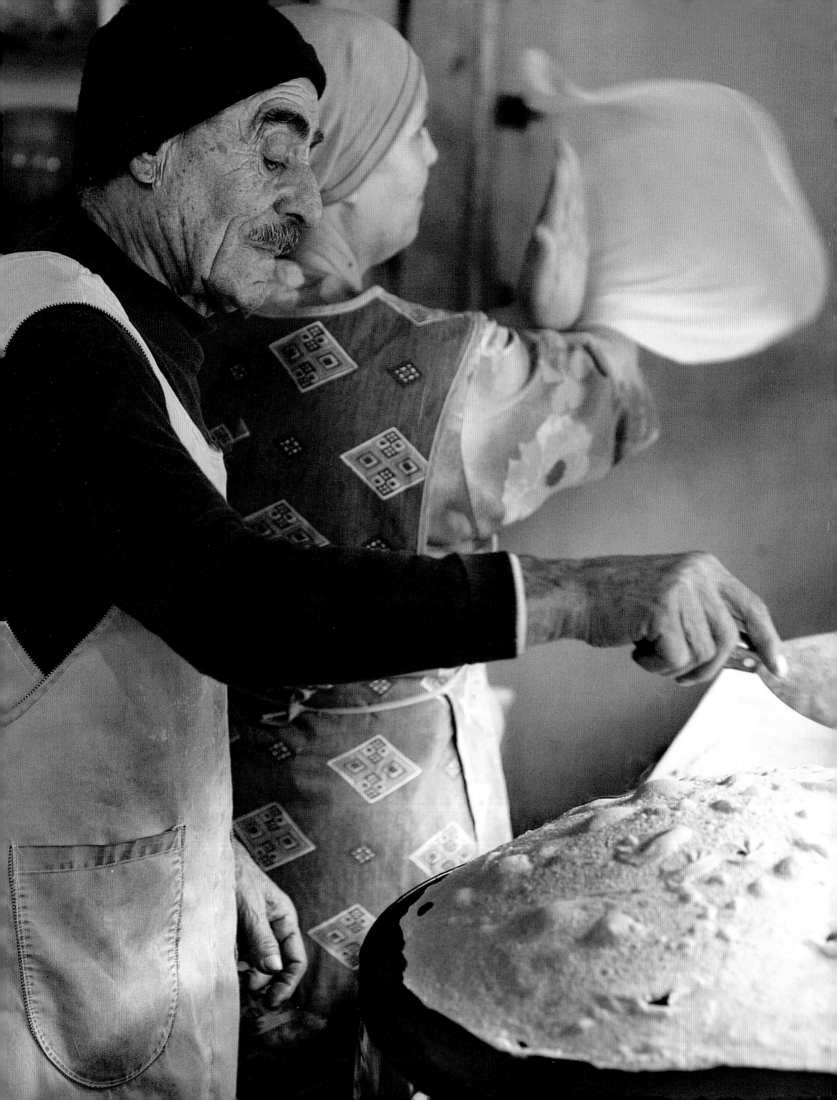

Paper–Thin Bread

Baking paper-thin bread (*khobz marquq*) is an occasion, a ritual, and an art in itself. Watching the ceremony of bread-making unravel before you is captivating. But before actually baking the bread—traditionally on a metallic convex disc (*saj*)—there are several measures that need to be established.

It used to be that, before you could make bread, it was necessary to prepare your flour. The harvested wheat was washed, dried in the sun, and preserved in wooden boxes. It was ground gradually at a local mill according to one's needs. In some remote villages, families still gather their wheat harvest to make their own flour. Others purchase a portion of a neighbor's harvest for their yearly consumption.

To make the dough, traditionally, the woman of the household kneels in front of a huge copper basin, carefully sifting the flour into it. Next to her, in a small glass, the yeast is dissolved into a small amount of lukewarm water, or she may use a homemade starter (*tarbayeh*, a piece of dough kept aside and fermented from the previous day) in place of yeast. According to Christian traditions, the first starter of the year is made on the sixth of January on the Christian Feast of the Epiphany. It is hung under a tree for three consecutive days to be blessed, then is mixed into the flour with salt.

When large quantities of dough are prepared, it is hard work mixing the ingredients to create soft dough. Kneading may take one hour for a 44-pound (20kg) batch. The woman sprinkles flour on the basin to prevent dough from sticking to its surface. When a uniform ball of dough is formed, the woman draws a cross on it or speaks the word "*Allah*" to bless her work.

The dough is left to rise for several hours under a damp white cloth (*mizar*). If the weather is hot, one to two hours is sufficient. When the weather is cold, the dough is left overnight to rise. The next step is to make small balls with the dough that will be individually patted to make the paper-thin bread. These are rolled in cornmeal, which gives the bread flavor and texture. The dough is left to rise for a second time, ranging from half an hour to two hours, depending, once more, on weather conditions.

In the summer, the underside of a convex metal disc (*saj*) is heated in a sheltered spot outdoors using dry pieces of wood or an apparatus that distributes gas through a metallic ring. Usually, the woman sits on the floor in front of a low wooden table (*tablieh*). She pats, presses, and shapes the dough on this table with a quick motion of the hands. She then tosses the patted dough from one hand to the other. The tempo increases as a wide circular shape develops. This action makes the dough paper-thin. The large circle of dough is placed on a cushion (*kara*) and is slowly stretched and tucked into an even, circular shape. She then flips the dough on the convex disc to bake for one to two minutes. As it becomes a light brown color, it is peeled off and placed upon a cloth-lined basket or a clean table. The procedure is repeated until all the dough is baked. After the bread cools, the sheets are folded neatly into quarters and stored.

It is not uncommon for a woman to set aside some dough to make smaller and thicker pieces of bread called *talamieh*. Some are stuffed with the family's favorite filling such as *kishk*, *labneh*, or ground meat. The stuffing is incorporated into the dough and made into thicker flat discs. These pies are cooked evenly on both sides. Others are soaked in meat drippings from the family dinner or from the preparation of meat preserve (*awarma*). The dough can also be dipped in various types of herbs such as mint, sage, chives, oregano, or basil.

I make a special pie with a combination of sautéed garlic, cilantro, and olive oil. I dip the dough in this mixture, then cook it on the convex disc. A woman from the west of the Beqa' Valley once told me with nostalgia that her grandmother used to leave pieces of dough to make her a bread shaped like a cow's head. She called it *ayn el bakar* meaning "eyes of the cow." With a little imagination and a flair for the right flavors, you can make your own creation.

◄ Preparing paper-thin
bread is an art in itself.

Paper-Thin Bread

أذن مرقوق

Khobz marquq

½ cup (13oz / 360g) of whole-wheat (whole-grain) flour

1 cup (5oz / 150g) of white bread (strong) flour

1 teaspoon of salt

1 teaspoon of active dry yeast or a piece of leavened starter from the preceding batch of bread

1¼ cups (300ml) of lukewarm water (body temperature is best)

¼ teaspoon of orange blossom water for extra flavor (optional)

2 tablespoons of cornmeal

1. Measure and sift flours and salt into a bowl. It is important to mix the dry ingredients first.

2. Dissolve the active dry yeast in the water (a yeast starter does not need to be dissolved).

3. In a large bowl, gradually beat the flour into the yeast mixture. Knead the mixture to make a soft dough. Add the orange blossom water, if using. You might need to add 1 or 2 tablespoons of water to the dough depending on the texture of the flour.

4. Tip the dough on to a lightly floured surface and knead for 5 to 10 minutes until smooth and elastic. (If you are using a stand mixer or food processor, run the machine for 1 minute. Start at a low speed, and then gradually turn up the speed. Always stand close to the machine while it is running.)

5. Place the dough in a large bowl dusted with extra flour. Cover the bowl with a damp dish towel and leave to rise in a warm place for 1½ to 2 hours, or until doubled in bulk.

6. Punch down the dough. On a floured surface, shape into a log. Pinch off the dough to form 5 to 10 equal-sized balls. Roll them in the cornmeal. If necessary, re-flour the bowl and leave balls to rise for an additional half-hour.

7. On a clean counter or a small wooden table, punch down each ball with your hands in a circular motion. Pick up the patted piece of dough. Shift it from one hand to the other in a quick motion in order to stretch it.

8. Preheat a large cast-iron griddle, crepe pan, or convex disc (*saj*). Stretch the dough over a cushion (*kara*) the size of your heat source. Tuck in the edges of the dough around the cushion. Flip the cushion, placing the stretched dough on your heat source.

9. Cook for 1 to 2 minutes, depending on heat source. Your bread is finished when a slightly brown color appears and the bread hardens. Be very careful not to let the bread burn.

10. Carefully peel off the bread and set to cool on a large tabletop or a large cloth-lined woven basket. Lightly spray your heat source with water and wipe away any debris.

11. Stack the finished bread, one on top of the other. To prevent drying, cover with a large cloth or plastic wrap. When cool, fold the circle in two; then fold again to create a triangular form. Store in airtight plastic bags. The bread will keep for one week in summer and approximately two weeks in winter or if refrigerated.

▶ Every Saturday morning, Oum Nazira, in the village of Lerad in the Kesserouan, prepares a huge batch of paper-thin bread to sell to neighbors.

Yields about 5–10 large sheets of bread, depending on the size of your heat source.

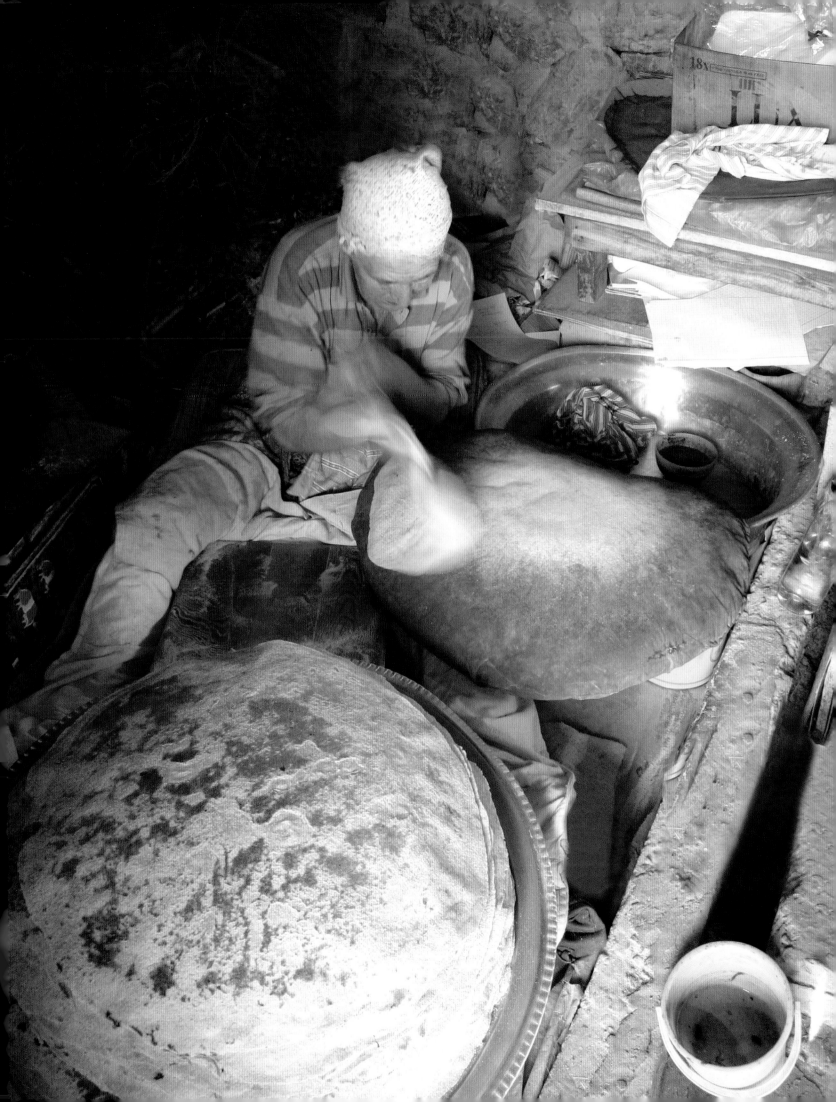

Wild
Thyme

الزعتر البري

Za'tar

Wild Thyme Mixture

Wild Thyme Pie

Wild Thyme with Fresh Vegetables

Wild Thyme with Red Pepper Paste

Wild Thyme Pie with Whole-Wheat
Flour and Bulgar Dough

Wild Thyme Pie with Walnuts

Light Wild Thyme Pie

Wild Thyme Mixture

Khaltet al- za'tar

خلطة الزعتر

Wild thyme, or *za'tar*, is found on hilltops and mountains all over Lebanon. *Za'tar* is also the name of an herb mixture that is most popularly enjoyed on *man'oushé* or with bread dipped in olive oil. According to mothers in Lebanon, eating *za'tar* makes you wiser. Before a quiz, children are often given *za'tar* because it is said to stimulate the memory. Regardless of its credibility, the adage is part of Lebanese culture. You can find *za'tar* in Middle Eastern grocery stores, but to make one's own mixture is very satisfying. It can involve everyone in the family. You can halve or quarter this recipe.

MIXTURE FOR MAN'OUSHÉ

7½ cups (2lb / 1kg) of ground, dried wild thyme (*za'tar*)

1½ cups (½lb / 225g) of sesame seeds (uncooked)

3 cups (1½lb / 400g) of ground sumac

¼ cup (2oz / 50g) of salt

MIXTURE FOR DIPPING

7½ cups (2lb / 1kg) of ground *za'tar*

1½ cups (½lb / 225g) of sesame seeds (toasted)

3 cups (1½lb / 400g) of ground sumac

½ cup (2oz / 50g) of salt

Note: In different parts of the Middle East, the name *za'tar* can refer to a range of wild herbs used to make *za'tar* mixture—including some varieties of thyme, oregano, hyssop, and even mint, depending on what grows regionally.

Picking
Wild thyme, or *za'tar*, is easy to find growing on the hilltops and mountains of Lebanon. The plant is distinctive and gives off a strong fragrance; let your nose be your guide. To harvest it, use sharp scissors or shears and cut the plant without pulling up the roots. If it doesn't grow wild in your region, use your favorite variety of thyme, or a combination of herbs in the same family, such as thyme, oregano, and marjoram.

Drying
Hang the sprigs in a warm, dry spot. It is preferable to keep them out of direct sunlight, which will scorch the leaves.

Separating
Separate the *za'tar* leaves, removing the stems, and cleaning off debris.

Grinding
In the past, the *za'tar* was reduced to a fine powder by grinding the dried plant with the hands. It was then pounded in a stone mortar. Today, many people take their *za'tar* to a mill to have it finely ground. You can grind it in a spice grinder or food processor, then pass it through a fine sieve.

Mixing
Combine the ground *za'tar*, sumac, sesame seeds, and salt and mix well.

Storing
Store the *za'tar* mixture in airtight containers with a couple of bay leaves to deter insects. It should stay fresh for up to a year.

▶ "Oum Tony" from Sourat in Batroun selecting wild thyme.

زعتر Wild Thyme Pie

Man'oushé bi-za'tar

This is the traditional way to prepare *man'oushé*. I prefer to use the combination of olive and vegetable oil for a lighter flavor.

Prepare the dough on page 42.

1 dough recipe (see p. 42)

½ cup (2oz / 60g) of wild thyme mixture (*za'tar*, see p. 54)

½ cup (120ml) of olive oil (or a mixture of olive and vegetable oil)

1. In a bowl, mix the wild thyme mixture with the oil until smooth.

2. If you are using a cast-iron crepe pan, griddle, or convex disc (*saj*), preheat over high heat. Heat the dough until small bubbles form; then lower the heat and spread on the topping. Cook until the bottom is slightly golden and the edges are crisp, about 3 to 5 minutes, depending on the heat source. Lightly spray the cooking surface with water between pies, and wipe away any debris.

   If you are using a conventional oven, preheat the oven to 400°F (200°C / Gas mark 6). Using the back of a spoon, spread the mixture over the prepared dough, leaving about ½in (1cm) of exposed dough at the edges. For more even distribution, use your fingertips. Bake for 7 to 10 minutes on the bottom shelf until the edges are slightly golden, watching carefully so they don't burn.

3. Serve the pies hot.

 Yields 4 pies.

🧁 *Cook's Tip:* Garnishes for the *man'oushé* can include fresh mint leaves, cucumbers, tomatoes, pickles, or olives. Some people even like to eat their *man'oushé* with a tablespoon of strained yogurt (*labneh*, see p. 85).

▲ Hannah enjoying *man'oushé* in her backyard in Bhamdoun.

◀ The *man'oushé* in all its splendor.

Wild Thyme Pie with Fresh Vegetables

Man'oushé bi-za'tar wa khodra

زعتر وخضرة

The addition of vegetables makes a delicious variation. You can use all of them together, just the tomato and onion, or each one separately.

Prepare the dough on page 42.

1 dough recipe (see p. 42)

½ cup (2oz / 60g) of wild thyme mixture (*za'tar*, see p. 54)

1 medium tomato, finely chopped

1 medium onion, finely chopped

½ green bell pepper, finely chopped (optional)

½ cup (120ml) of olive oil (or a mixture of olive and vegetable oil)

Mint leaves and pickled turnips (*lifit*), to garnish (optional)

1. In a bowl, combine the wild thyme mixture, chopped vegetables, and oil.

2. If you are using a cast-iron crepe pan, griddle, or convex disc (*saj*), preheat over high heat. Heat the dough until small bubbles form; then lower the heat and spread on the topping. Cook until the bottom is slightly golden and the edges are crisp, about 3 to 5 minutes, depending on the heat source. Lightly spray the cooking surface with water between pies, and wipe away any debris.

   If you are using a conventional oven, preheat the oven to 400°F (200°C / Gas mark 6). Using the back of a spoon, spread the mixture over the prepared dough, leaving about ½in (1cm) of exposed dough at the edges. For more even distribution, use your fingertips. Bake for 7 to 10 minutes on the bottom shelf until the edges are slightly golden, watching carefully so they don't burn.

3. Serve the pies hot, garnished with mint leaves and pickled turnips, if desired.

Yields 4 pies.

▲ *Man'oushé* break for Albert, my son.

▶ Pickled turnips (*lifit*) add a curious flavor to the *man'oushé*.

Wild Thyme Pie with Red Pepper Paste

زعتر وربّ الحرّ

Za'tar wa ribb al-harr

"Baddak tla'eh hadan yakila!" meaning: "You have to find someone who dares eat this *man'oushé!"* shouted Said the baker, as I was walking away on a busy street in Ashrafieh in Beirut, after giving me this spicy recipe. I dare you!

Prepare the dough on page 42.

1 dough recipe (see p. 42)

½ cup (2oz / 60g) of wild thyme mixture (*za'tar,* see p. 54)

1 medium onion, finely chopped

1 medium tomato, finely chopped

1 tablespoon of red pepper paste (see p. 153)

½ cup (120ml) of olive oil (or a mixture of olive and vegetable oil)

1. In a bowl, combine the wild thyme mixture with the onion, tomato, red pepper paste, and oil (or you may choose to add the red pepper paste separately).

2. If you are using a cast-iron crepe pan, griddle, or convex disc (*saj*), preheat over high heat. Heat the dough until small bubbles form; then lower the heat and spread on the topping. Cook until the bottom is slightly golden and the edges are crisp, about 3 to 5 minutes, depending on the heat source. Lightly spray the cooking surface with water between pies, and wipe away any debris.

   If you are using a conventional oven, preheat the oven to 400°F (200°C / Gas mark 6). Using the back of a spoon, spread the mixture over the prepared dough, leaving about ½in (1cm) of exposed dough at the edges. For more even distribution, use your fingertips. Bake for 7 to 10 minutes on the bottom shelf until the edges are slightly golden, watching carefully so they don't burn.

3. Serve the pies hot.

 Yields 4 pies.

▲ Red pepper paste adds a striking color and a spicy flavor to the *man'oushé.*

◀ An authentic wood-
burning convex disc
in a quaint traditional
bakery.

▶ Spreading za'tar evenly
can be done with the
back of a spoon.

Wild Thyme Pie with Whole-Wheat Flour and Bulgar Dough

Jreesh

In Lebanon, anise seeds are usually used to make a drink called *yansun*. Used here, they give the dough a strong flavor. I like to use them sparingly; you may prefer more. I visited the south of Lebanon and spoke to a woman in the region of Nabatieh, who gave me this recipe. She also makes a version using semolina instead of bulgar. She spoke of the recipe with melancholy, stating that this was her poor mother's recipe.

THE DOUGH

1 cup (5oz / 150g) of bulgar (cracked wheat, *burghul*)

1½ teaspoons of active dry yeast

1 cup (250ml) of lukewarm water (body temperature is best)

3¼ cups (13oz / 375g) of whole-wheat (whole-grain) flour

2 teaspoons of salt

1 tablespoon of vegetable oil

1 tablespoon of whole anise seeds

1 teaspoon of ground anise seeds

1 teaspoon of ground mahlab (optional)

THE TOPPING

¾ cup (3½oz / 100g) of wild thyme mixture (*za'tar*, see p. 54)

¾ cup (175ml) of olive oil
(or a mixture of olive and vegetable oil)

1. Soak the bulgar in water, to cover, for half an hour. This will add moisture to the dough; therefore less water is needed in the dough mixture.

2. Dissolve the yeast in the water and set aside.

3. In a large bowl, mix the flour, salt, oil, and spices.

4. Drain the bulgar well and add it to the flour mixture. Pour the yeast water in the center and mix until soft dough is formed.

5. Transfer the dough to a work surface and knead for 5 to 10 minutes.

6. Follow steps 6 to 10 on p. 42.

7. In a bowl, mix the wild thyme mixture with the oil until well blended.

8. If you are using a cast-iron crepe pan, griddle, or convex disc (*saj*), preheat over high heat. Heat the dough until small bubbles form; then lower the heat and spread on the topping. Cook until the bottom is slightly golden and the edges are crisp, about 3 to 5 minutes, depending on the heat source. Lightly spray the cooking surface with water between pies, and wipe away any debris.

   If you are using a conventional oven, preheat the oven to 400°F (200°C / Gas mark 6). Using the back of a spoon, spread the mixture over the prepared dough, leaving about ½in (1cm) of exposed dough at the edges. For more even distribution, use your fingertips. Bake for 7 to 10 minutes on the bottom shelf until the edges are slightly golden, watching carefully so they don't burn.

9. Serve the pies hot.

 Yields 4 pies.

Wild Thyme Pie with Walnuts

Za'tar wa jawz

A woman came into the Khalifeh bakery in Ballouneh with this flavorful topping. The aroma and taste were so appreciated that this pie became part of the menu.

Prepare the dough on p. 42

1 dough recipe (see p. 42)

½ cup (2oz / 60g) of wild thyme mixture (*za'tar*, see p. 54)

1 tablespoon of Aleppo thyme mixture

1 medium onion, finely chopped

½ cup (2oz / 60g) of finely-chopped walnuts

1 tablespoon of red pepper paste (see p. 153)

1 teaspoon of cumin

½ cup (120ml) of olive oil (or a mixture of olive and vegetable oil)

1. In a bowl, mix both thyme mixtures with the onion, nuts, red pepper paste, cumin, and the oil.

2. If you are using a cast-iron crepe pan, griddle, or convex disc (*saj*), preheat over high heat. Heat the dough until small bubbles form; then lower the heat and spread on the topping. Cook until the bottom is slightly golden and the edges are crisp, about 3 to 5 minutes, depending on the heat source. Lightly spray the cooking surface with water between pies, and wipe away any debris.

   If you are using a conventional oven, preheat the oven to 400°F (200°C / Gas mark 6). Using the back of a spoon, spread the mixture over the prepared dough, leaving about ½in (1cm) of exposed dough at the edges. For more even distribution, use your fingertips. Bake for 7 to 10 minutes on the bottom shelf until the edges are slightly golden, watching carefully so they don't burn.

3. Serve the pies hot.

 Yields 4 pies.

Light Wild Thyme Pie

Man'oushé bi-za'tar "light"

For those who can't live without *man'oushé*, but want to watch those calories!

Prepare the dough on page 42, replacing the bread flour with whole-wheat flour.
Divide the dough into 6 equal pieces and roll very thinly.

1 modified dough recipe (see p. 42)

½ cup (2oz / 60g) of wild thyme mixture (*za'tar*, see p. 54)

½ cup (120ml) of olive oil

Fresh mint, cucumber slices, and tomato slices, to garnish (optional)

1. Tap the dough with your fingertips or poke holes with a fork to prevent air pockets from forming.

2. In a bowl, mix the thyme mixture with the olive oil until smooth.

3. Cook the dough according to your preferred cooking method. If you are using a cast-iron crepe pan, griddle, or convex disc, preheat over high heat. Cook the dough until the bottom is slightly golden and the edges are crisp, about 3 to 5 minutes, depending on the heat source. Lightly spray the cooking surface with water between pies, and wipe away any debris.

   If you are using a conventional oven, preheat the oven to 425°F (220°C / Gas mark 7). Bake the dough for 5 to 7 minutes on the bottom shelf until the edges are slightly golden, watching carefully so they don't burn.

4. Using the back of a spoon, thinly spread the mixture over the cooked dough, leaving about ½in (1cm) of exposed dough at the edges. For more even distribution, use your fingertips.

5. Garnish with low-calorie ingredients like fresh mint leaves, cucumbers, and tomatoes.

◀ Maria, a Lebanese beauty!

▼ Everyone is hungry and in a hurry at Barbar's, located on Spears Street.

 Yields 6 pies.

Cook's Tip: If you make your own wild thyme mixture (*za'tar*), you can omit the sesame seeds to further reduce the calorie intake.

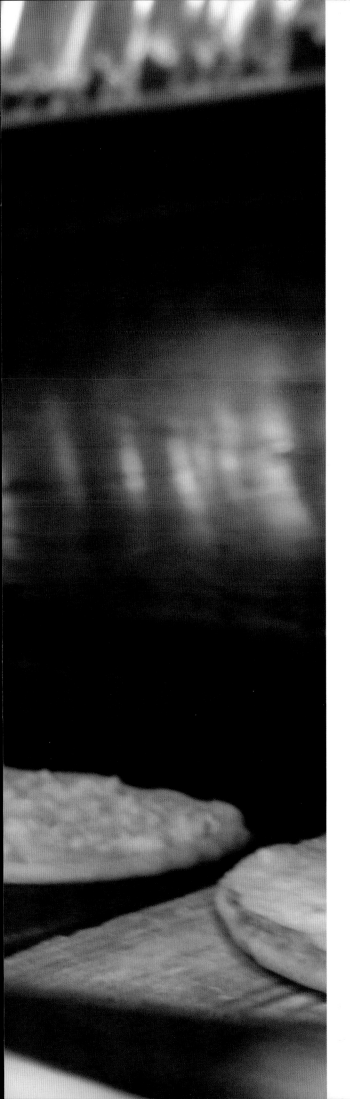

Cheese
الجبنة

Jibneh

Cheese Pie

Supreme Cheese Pie

Hot Cheese Pie

Cheese Pie with Vegetables

Spiced Cheese Balls

Spiced Cheese Pie

Spiced Cheese Pie with White Cheese

Bulgari Cheese Pie

Feta Cheese Pie

Kashkaval Cheese Pie

Strained Yogurt Pie

Cooked Strained Yogurt Pie

Whey Cheese Pie

Cheese Pie

Jibneh

After the *man'oushé bi-za'tar* (wild thyme pie), *jibneh* (cheese) is the most popular pie ordered in the Lebanese street corner bakery. It is usually made with a white cheese called *'akkawi*. The cheese is cut into even squares and preserved in salted water. Firm mozzarella is an acceptable substitute.

Prepare the dough on page 42.

1 dough recipe (see p. 42)

4 cups (1lb / 500g) of grated *'akkawi* cheese

1. *'Akkawi* cheese is very salty. To reduce the salt content, soak the grated cheese in water overnight. Change the water two or three times, if possible. If time does not permit, soak the grated cheese for a couple of hours, then run cold water over the cheese in a colander. Drain well before using.

2. If you are using a cast-iron crepe pan, griddle, or convex disc (*saj*), preheat over high heat. Heat the dough until small bubbles form; then lower the heat and melt the cheese in the middle of the dough for about 30 seconds, before spreading it evenly on the dough. This method will prevent cheese from running onto the cooking surface. Cook until the bottom is slightly golden and the edges are crisp, about 3 to 5 minutes, depending on the heat source. Lightly spray the cooking surface with water between pies, and wipe away any debris.

   If you are using a conventional oven, preheat the oven to 400°F (200°C / Gas mark 6). Sprinkle the cheese evenly onto the prepared dough, leaving about ½in (1cm) of exposed dough at the edges. Bake for 7 to 10 minutes on the bottom shelf until the dough is cooked and the cheese is slightly golden, watching carefully to make sure it does not burn.

3. Serve the pies hot.

 Yields 4 pies.

Cook's Tip: You can add 1 teaspoon of dried mint and 1 tablespoon of oil to the cheese before cooking, or add a sprinkle dried red pepper powder on top, if desired.

◀ *Man'oushé bi-jibneh cooked in a wood-burning oven with olive tree branches.*

▶ *The hot cheese just melts in your mouth.*

Supreme Cheese Pie

Jibneh tlet anwa'

جبنة ٣ أنواع

A delight for cheese lovers! This combination makes a rich and delicious pie.

Prepare the dough on page 42.

1 dough recipe (see p. 42)

2 cups (8oz / 240g) of 'akkawi cheese

1 cup (4oz / 120g) of halloumi cheese

1 cup (4oz / 120g) of Bulgari or feta cheese

1. *'Akkawi* cheese is very salty. To reduce the salt content, soak the grated cheese in water overnight. Change the water two or three times, if possible. If time does not permit, soak the grated cheese for a couple of hours, then run cold water over the cheese in a colander. Drain well before using.

2. Cut the halloumi cheese into cubes. If the halloumi is too salty, follow the same procedure as for the *'akkawi* cheese.

3. Mix the *'akkawi* and halloumi with the crumbled Bulgari or feta cheese.

4. If you are using a cast-iron crepe pan, griddle, or convex disc (*saj*), preheat over high heat. Heat the dough until small bubbles form; then lower the heat and melt the cheese in the middle of the dough for about 30 seconds, before spreading it evenly on the dough. This method will prevent cheese from running onto the cooking surface. Cook until the bottom is slightly golden and the edges are crisp, about 3 to 5 minutes, depending on the heat source. Lightly spray the cooking surface with water between pies, and wipe away any debris.

   If you are using a conventional oven, preheat the oven to 400°F (200°C / Gas mark 6). Sprinkle the cheese evenly onto the prepared dough, leaving about ½in (1cm) of exposed dough at the edges. Bake for 7 to 10 minutes on the bottom shelf until the dough is cooked and the cheese is slightly golden, watching carefully to make sure it does not burn.

5. Serve the pies hot.

Yields 4 pies.

Cook's Tip: You can sprinkle 1 teaspoon of raw sesame seeds onto the cheese pie before cooking, or a sprinkle of Aleppo pepper, paprika, or hot red pepper flakes.

▲ Cold running water rinses out excess salt from the cheese.

▶ Khan el Franj, the ancient souk in Saida.

◀ Hot and spicy pies cooked in Mr. Gabaret's intricately decorated oven.

▶ Satisfying morning hunger with great appetite. *Sahteyn!*

Hot Cheese Pie

Jibneh wa harr

This recipe was given to me by Mr. Gabaret, who owns one of the oldest bakeries in Bourj-Hamoud, Beirut's Armenian district. This pie is absolutely fabulous!

Prepare the dough on page 42.

1 dough recipe (see p. 42)

3 cups (12½oz / 360g) of 'akkawi cheese

2 medium tomatoes, finely chopped

1 medium onion, finely chopped

1 teaspoon to 1 tablespoon of hot red pepper paste (see p. 153), or to taste

1 teaspoon to 1 tablespoon of tomato paste, or to taste

Pinch of cumin

½ teaspoon of salt

2 tablespoons of vegetable oil

1. 'Akkawi cheese is very salty. To reduce the salt content, soak the grated cheese in water overnight. Change the water two or three times, if possible. If time does not permit, soak the grated cheese for a couple of hours, then run cold water over the cheese in a colander. Drain well before using.

2. In a bowl, combine the 'akkawi cheese with the onion and tomatoes. Add the red pepper paste, tomato paste, cumin, and salt. Pour in the oil. Mix well.

3. If you are using a cast-iron crepe pan, griddle, or convex disc (*saj*), preheat over high heat. Heat the dough until small bubbles form; then lower the heat and melt the cheese in the middle of the dough for about 30 seconds, before spreading it evenly on the dough. This method will prevent cheese from running onto the cooking surface. Cook until the bottom is slightly golden and the edges are crisp, about 3 to 5 minutes, depending on the heat source. Lightly spray the cooking surface with water between pies, and wipe away any debris.

   If you are using a conventional oven, preheat the oven to 400°F (200°C / Gas mark 6). Sprinkle the cheese evenly onto the prepared dough, leaving about ½in (1cm) of exposed dough at the edges. Bake for 7 to 10 minutes on the bottom shelf until the dough is cooked and the cheese is slightly golden, watching carefully to make sure it does not burn.

4. Serve the pies hot.

 Yields 4 pies.

☕ *Cook's Tip:* You can replace the tomatoes, cumin, and red pepper paste with half a bunch of parsley and a pinch of red pepper powder. This pie can be shaped into a log: roll the dough into a long, thin rectangle, spread it with the topping, and fold the long sides carefully over the topping, leaving a thin slit in the middle. This is the new craze in Lebanese bakeries!

Cheese Pie with Vegetables

Jibneh wa khodra

جبنة وخضرة

The addition of fresh vegetables makes this pie tasty and healthful.

Prepare the dough on page 42.

1 dough recipe (see p. 42)

3 cups (13oz / 360g) of 'akkawi cheese

1 large onion, finely chopped

3 medium tomatoes, finely chopped

1 medium red or green bell pepper, finely chopped

Pinch of sumac

½ teaspoon of salt

½ teaspoon of black pepper

¼ cup (60ml) of olive oil

1. *'Akkawi* cheese is very salty. To reduce the salt content, soak the grated cheese in water overnight. Change the water two or three times, if possible. If time does not permit, soak the grated cheese for a couple of hours, then run cold water over the cheese in a colander. Drain well before using.

2. In a mixing bowl, combine the chopped onion, tomatoes, and bell pepper. Sprinkle with sumac. Add salt and pepper, mix well, and add the oil.

3. If you are using a cast-iron crepe pan, griddle, or convex disc (*saj*), preheat over high heat. Heat the dough until small bubbles form, before spreading the topping. Cook until the bottom is slightly golden and the edges are crisp, about 3 to 5 minutes, depending on the heat source. Lightly spray the cooking surface with water between pies, and wipe away any debris.

   If you are using a conventional oven, preheat the oven to 400°F (200°C / Gas mark 6). Spread the vegetable mixture evenly onto the prepared dough, leaving about ½in (1cm) of exposed dough at the edges. Top with the 'akkawi cheese. Bake for 7 to 10 minutes on the bottom shelf until the dough is cooked and the cheese is slightly golden, watching carefully to make sure it does not burn.

4. Serve the pies hot.

 Yields 4 pies.

Cook's Tip: You can add 1 or 2 crushed garlic cloves to the mixture.

Spiced Cheese Balls

Shankleesh

شنكليش

Shankleesh, known as peasant's cheese, is an important component of the traditional *mezze*. It is strong-tasting and very flavorful. Making *shankleesh* is a craft typical of the mountains of Lebanon. Fresh drained curd is mixed with salt and spices and shaped into balls. It is dried in the sun for three days, then stored in airtight containers and left to ferment for up to a month, before being rolled in wild thyme mixture (*za'tar*). *Shankleesh* can be made from cow's, sheep's, or goat's milk yogurt, all producing different flavors. This recipe can be multiplied, as desired.

FOR EACH BALL, USE

2¼lb (1kg) of low-fat yogurt

⅓ cup (3½oz / 100g) of salt

1 tablespoon of dried red pepper powder (optional)

½ teaspoon of seven-spice or allspice (optional)

3–4 cups (12–4oz / 350–475g) of wild thyme mixture (*za'tar*, see p. 54)

1. Pour the yogurt into a large cooking pan and bring it slowly to a boil. Stirring constantly, boil until the curds and whey start to separate and the curds sink to the bottom in small white lumps. Leave to cool.

2. Line a large bowl with sterilized cheesecloth (muslin), making sure there is lots of excess fabric hanging over the sides. Once the curds are cool, pour them into the lined bowl. Tie the ends of the cloth together around the curds and secure with a string. Hang it over the sink or a bowl in the refrigerator to drain overnight or until the contents are firm. You may need to drain for up to 2 days. Once firm, the curds should easily break away from the cloth.

3. Add salt, ½ cup of wild thyme mixture, and the spices, if using and mix thoroughly.

4. Form the curds into a ball, roughly the size of a tennis ball, and place on a tray lined with a clean, sterilized cloth.

5. Cover with another piece of cloth to protect against insects or debris. Leave the cheese ball to dry, out of direct sunlight, for 3 to 4 days in the summer or 8 to 10 days in the winter, depending on weather conditions, changing the cloth lining the tray every few hours (this will ensure the balls dry completely).

6. Once dried, leave the cheese ball to mature in a clay jar or other airtight container away from light for 7 to 10 days for a mild-flavored cheese or 30 to 40 days for a strong, sharp-flavored cheese. A cottony mold will cover the cheese.

7. Rinse the ball under cold running water and roll it in the wild thyme mixture until completely covered.

8. Serve the spiced cheese ball, crushed, with finely chopped onion, tomato, and green pepper, topped with olive oil, or use to make spiced cheese pies (see pp. 78–9). These can be stored in the refrigerator for up to 3 to 4 months, if covered with plastic wrap.

Yields 1 large cheese ball

▶ *Shankleesh* in the form of a ball, coated in wild thyme mixture.

Spiced Cheese Pie

Shankleesh

Rahbeh, a village situated in northern Lebanon, is famous for its *shankleesh* production. Two important factors make the cheese special: Rahbeh producers use only cow's milk, and they use traditional ripening methods. Jamileh Gerges Yussef, a woman from Rahbeh, was kind enough to show me the old-fashioned technique for making *shankleesh*. If you can't find it ready-made, make your own using the recipe on p. 77.

Prepare the dough on page 42.

1 dough recipe (see p. 42)

1 large spiced cheese ball (*shankleesh*, see p. 77)

1 medium onion, finely chopped

2 medium tomatoes, finely chopped

¼ cup (60ml) of oil (a mixture of olive and vegetable oil)

½ teaspoon of salt

Pinch of red pepper flakes

¼ cup (60ml) of olive oil, to serve (optional)

1. Cut the cheese into cubes; it will crumble.

2. In a mixing bowl, combine the cheese with chopped onion and tomato and add the mixed oil. Sprinkle with salt and red pepper flakes.

3. If you are using a cast-iron crepe pan, griddle, or convex disc (*saj*), preheat over high heat. Heat the dough until small bubbles form before spreading the topping. Cook until the bottom is slightly golden and the edges are crisp, about 3 to 5 minutes, depending on the heat source. Lightly spray the cooking surface with water between pies, and wipe away any debris.

   If you are using a conventional oven, preheat the oven to 400°F (200°C / Gas mark 6). Spread the topping evenly onto the prepared dough, leaving about ½in (1cm) of exposed dough at the edges. Bake for 7 to 10 minutes on the bottom shelf until the dough is cooked and edges are slightly golden, watching carefully to make sure it does not burn.

4. For extra flavor, drizzle 1 tablespoon of olive oil on each cooked pie.

5. Serve the pies hot.

 Yields 4 pies.

🎩 *Cook's Tip:* You can replace the red pepper flakes with 1 finely diced red or green bell pepper. Or simply add a bunch of fresh mint, chopped, to the mixture.

► I invite you to entertain your family and friends with a *saj* party; all you need is a piece of dough and some basic toppings.

Spiced Cheese Pie with White Cheese

شنكليش وعكاوي

Shankleesh wa 'akkawi

Annie Kabakian, a very dear woman whom I met during my culinary journey in 'Anjar, first taught me to make *shankleesh*, known as peasant's cheese, and an important component of the traditional *mezze*. In the past, because of lack of refrigeration, this cheese was dried completely and stored in clay jars for months to ferment. Before use, it had to be pounded in a mortar (*jurn*). It was often sprinkled on salads and various other dishes. The mixture of *'akkawi* cheese with the *shankleesh* makes a lighter pie, but still preserves the strong flavor of the latter.

Prepare the dough on page 42.

1 dough recipe (see p. 42)

1 medium spiced cheese ball (*shankleesh*, see p. 77)

1 cup (4oz / 120g) of *'akkawi* cheese

1 medium onion, finely chopped

2 medium tomatoes, finely chopped

2 tablespoons of wild thyme mixture (*za'tar*, see p. 54)

¼ cup (60ml) of olive oil

1. *'Akkawi* cheese is very salty. To reduce the salt content, soak the grated cheese in water overnight. Change the water two or three times, if possible. If time does not permit, soak the grated cheese for a couple of hours, then run cold water over the cheese in a colander. Drain well before using.

2. Cut the *shankleesh* into cubes. The cheese will crumble.

3. In a mixing bowl, combine the drained *'akkawi* cheese, crumbled *shankleesh*, chopped onion and tomatoes, and the wild thyme mixture. Pour in the oil. Mix well.

4. If you are using a cast-iron crepe pan, griddle, or convex disc (*saj*), preheat over high heat. Heat the dough until small bubbles form before spreading the topping. Cook until the bottom is slightly golden and the edges are crisp, about 3 to 5 minutes, depending on the heat source. Lightly spray the cooking surface with water between pies, and wipe away any debris.

   If you are using a conventional oven, preheat the oven to 400°F (200°C / Gas mark 6). Spread the topping evenly onto the prepared dough, leaving about ½in (1cm) of exposed dough at the edges. Bake for 7 to 10 minutes on the bottom shelf until the dough is cooked and edges are slightly golden, watching carefully to make sure it does not burn.

5. For extra flavor, drizzle 1 tablespoon of olive oil on each cooked pie.

6. Serve the pies hot.

 Yields 4 pies.

🍳 *Cook's tip:* You can add ½ green bell pepper, finely chopped, to the topping mixture.

▶ Bite-sized pies can be formed into crescents or circles.

◀ Sorting and chopping parsley is a strenuous effort.

Bulgari Cheese Pie

Bulghari

This pie can be made full-size and served as a meal, or bite-sized to be served as an hors-d'oeuvre.

Prepare the dough on page 42, dividing the dough into 4 equal parts to make regular pies, or 16–20 parts to make bite-sized pies (you can roll the dough out and cut out the pieces using a cookie cutter or glass). If making bite-sized pies, bake on a lightly-oiled baking tray for 15 to 20 minutes.

1 modified dough recipe (see p. 42)

3 cups (13oz / 375g) of Bulgari cheese

1 medium onion, finely chopped

3 tablespoons of finely-chopped parsley

1 tablespoon of finely-chopped mint

¼ cup (60ml) of oil (a mixture of olive and vegetable oil)

¼ cup (60ml) of olive oil (optional)

1. Cut the Bulgari cheese into cubes. The cheese will crumble.

2. In a mixing bowl, combine the cheese with the chopped onion, parsley, and mint. Pour in ¼ cup of oil and mix well.

3. If you are using a cast-iron crepe pan, griddle, or convex disc (*saj*), preheat over high heat. Heat the dough until small bubbles form, before spreading the topping. Cook until the bottom is slightly golden and the edges are crisp, about 3 to 5 minutes, depending on the heat source. Lightly spray the cooking surface with water between pies, and wipe away any debris.

   If you are using a conventional oven, preheat the oven to 400°F (200°C / Gas mark 6). Spread the topping evenly onto the prepared dough, leaving a crust of exposed dough at the edges. Bake for 7 to 10 minutes on the bottom shelf until the dough is cooked and edges are slightly golden, watching carefully to make sure they don't burn.

4. For larger pies, drizzle 1 tablespoon of olive oil on each cooked pie for extra flavor.

5. Let the pies cool before serving.

Yields 4 regular or 16–20 bite-sized pies.

Cook's tip: You can substitute the Bulgari cheese with Greek feta cheese, if desired.

Feta Cheese Pie

Feta

The combination of feta cheese with tomatoes and onions makes this pie refreshing and very tasty. This recipe is a favorite of mine during the hot summer months.

Prepare the dough on page 42.

1 dough recipe (see p. 42)

3 cups (13oz / 375g) of feta cheese, cubed

1 medium onion or a bunch of scallions (spring onions), finely chopped

2 medium tomatoes, chopped

¼ cup (60ml) of oil (a mixture of olive and vegetable oil)

¼ cup (60ml) of olive oil (optional)

1. Cut the feta cheese into cubes. The cheese will crumble.

2. In a bowl, combine the cheese with the chopped onion and tomatoes. Pour in ¼ cup of mixed oil and mix well.

3. If you are using a cast-iron crepe pan, griddle, or convex disc (*saj*), preheat over high heat. Heat the dough until small bubbles form before spreading the topping. Cook until the bottom is slightly golden and the edges are crisp, about 3 to 5 minutes, depending on the heat source. Lightly spray the cooking surface with water between pies, and wipe away any debris.

   If you are using a conventional oven, preheat the oven to 400°F (200°C / Gas mark 6). Spread the topping evenly onto the prepared dough, leaving about ½in (1cm) of exposed dough at the edges. Bake for 7 to 10 minutes on the bottom shelf until the dough is cooked and edges are slightly golden, watching carefully to make sure it does not burn.

4. For extra flavor, drizzle 1 tablespoon of olive oil on each cooked pie.

5. Serve the pies hot.

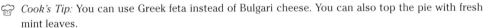 *Yields 4 pies.*

Cook's Tip: You can use Greek feta instead of Bulgari cheese. You can also top the pie with fresh mint leaves.

Kashkaval Cheese Pie

Ash'awan

Kashaval cheese is rich in flavor and very common in Lebanon. It is often served inside Arabic bread, topped with sliced cucumbers.

Prepare the dough on page 42.

1 dough recipe (see p. 42)

3 cups (10½oz / 300g) of coarsely grated kashkaval cheese

1. If you are using a cast-iron crepe pan, griddle, or convex disc (*saj*), preheat over high heat. Heat the dough until small bubbles form; then lower the heat, and melt the cheese in the middle of the dough for about 30 seconds, before spreading it evenly on the dough. This method will prevent cheese from running onto the cooking surface. Cook until the bottom is slightly golden and the edges are crisp, about 3 to 5 minutes, depending on the heat source. Lightly spray the cooking surface with water between pies, and wipe away any debris.

   If you are using a conventional oven, preheat the oven to 400°F (200°C / Gas mark 6). Sprinkle the cheese evenly onto the prepared dough, leaving about ½in (1cm) of exposed dough at the edges. Bake for 7 to 10 minutes on the bottom shelf until the dough is cooked and the cheese is slightly golden, watching carefully to make sure it does not burn.

2. Serve the pies hot.

 Yields 4 pies.

Strained Yogurt Pie
Labneh

Labneh (thick, strained yogurt) is one of the most popular cheeses in Lebanon. It is eaten during breakfast or dinner, and is an important part of the Lebanese *mezze*. The combination of fresh *labneh* with tomato, mint leaves, cucumber, and olives, all topped with olive oil is distinctly Lebanese.

Prepare the dough on page 42.

1 dough recipe (see p. 42)

1 cup (10oz / 280g) of strained yogurt (*labneh*, see below)

3 medium tomatoes, sliced

1 bunch of fresh mint

20 black or green olives

3 small cucumbers, sliced (optional)

¼ cup (60ml) of olive oil

Salt, to taste

1. Tap the dough with your fingertips or prick with a fork to prevent air pockets from forming.

2. If you are using a cast-iron crepe pan, griddle, or convex disc (*saj*), preheat over high heat. Cook each circle of dough until the bottom is slightly golden and the edges are crisp, about 3 to 5 minutes, depending on the heat source. Lightly spray the cooking surface with water between pies, and wipe away any debris.

   If you are using a conventional oven, preheat the oven to 425°F (220°C / Gas mark 7). Bake the dough for 5 to 7 minutes on the bottom shelf, watching carefully to make sure it does not burn.

3. Allow the bread discs to cool slightly before evenly spreading the *labneh* onto each one. Top with tomato slices, fresh mint leaves, olives, and cucumber slices, if using.

4. Drizzle 1 tablespoon of olive oil onto each pie and sprinkle with salt, if desired.

Yields 4 pies.

Cook's Tips: If you can't find strained yogurt (*labneh*), make your own: Mix 4 cups (2lb / 1kg) of plain Greek yogurt with 1 teaspoon of salt and pour onto the center of a large square of cheesecloth. Tie with string into a parcel and suspend over the sink (or a bowl in the refrigerator). Leave to drip overnight or until the yogurt thickens to the consistency of soft cream cheese. For a stronger flavor, you can use *labneh* made from goat's milk yogurt.

▶ A group of boys
(shabab) on Bliss
Street, a crowded
university district.

▶ Azar Bakery: za'tar,
cheese pie, meat pie,
spinach, kishk, pizza,
pastries, drinks.

لبنة بالفرن

Cooked Strained Yogurt Pie

Labneh bi'l forn

This pie is absolutely delicious! Add a pinch of red pepper powder or white pepper for extra flavor.

Prepare the dough on page 42, dividing the dough into 6 equal parts to make regular pies, or 16 parts to make bite-sized pies (you can roll the dough out and cut out the pieces using a cookie cutter or glass). If making bite-sized pies, bake on a lightly-oiled baking tray for 15 to 20 minutes.

1 modified dough recipe (see p. 42)

2 cups (15oz / 425g) of strained yogurt (*labneh*, see p. 85)

1 medium onion, finely chopped

3 tablespoons of finely-chopped fresh mint leaves

2 cloves of garlic, minced

2 tablespoons (30ml) of olive oil

½ teaspoon of salt (optional)

1. In a bowl, combine the *labneh*, onion, mint, and garlic; mix well. Pour in the olive oil, and sprinkle with salt, if needed.

2. Spread mixture onto the prepared dough, leaving about ½in (1cm) of exposed dough at the edges.

3. If you are using a cast-iron crepe pan, griddle, or convex disc (*saj*), preheat over high heat. Heat the dough until small bubbles form; then lower the heat and spread on the topping. Cook until the bottom is slightly golden and the edges are crisp, about 3 to 5 minutes, depending on the heat source. Lightly spray the cooking surface with water between pies, and wipe away any debris.

   If you are using a conventional oven, preheat the oven to 400°F (200°C / Gas mark 6). Using the back of a spoon, spread the mixture over the prepared dough, leaving about ½in (1cm) of exposed dough at the edges. Bake for 7 to 10 minutes on the bottom shelf until the edges are slightly golden, watching carefully so they don't burn.

4. Serve the pies hot.

 Yields 6 large pies or 16 bite-sized pies.

🧑‍🍳 *Cook's Tip:* Another way to make these pie is to fold the dough in half over the topping, forming a half-moon shape. This will prevent the cheese from drying out. Using a pastry brush, coat the pie with oil before cooking. Flip the pie over halfway through cooking.

فرن عانزاد

مشاقيش * جبنة

لحم بعجين * سبانخ

كشك * بيتزا معجنات

مرطبات

▲ In the mountaintop of
Warde in Faraya, Mrs. Khalil
prepares paper-thin bread.

▲ Mr. Khalil, a proud
shepherd, dressed in the
traditional Lebanese
attire, the *sherwal*.

▲ A mix of charcoal and
water is used to clean the
convex disc before use.

▶ This affectionate mountain
dweller prepares *talamieh*
for my children from the
last pieces of dough.

◄ A student passes by the nearest street corner bakery to have his breakfast.

Whey Cheese Pie

قريشة

Arisheh

Arisheh is a soft cheese made from whey. It resembles cottage cheese in appearance. If you can't find *arisheh*, you can substitute ricotta or your favorite whey cheese.

Prepare the dough on page 42.

1 dough recipe (see p. 42)

4 cups (1lb / 500g) of *arisheh*

½ cup of chopped scallions (spring onions)

1 tablespoon of dried mint or 1 bunch of fresh mint, chopped

1 teaspoon of red pepper paste (see p. 153) or 1 teaspoon of red pepper powder

½ cup (120ml) of olive oil (or a mixture of olive and vegetable oil)

Salt, to taste

1. In a bowl, combine the *arisheh* with the scallions, the dried mint, and the red pepper paste or powder.

2. If you are using a cast-iron crepe pan, griddle, or convex disc (*saj*), preheat over high heat. Heat the dough until small bubbles form; then lower the heat and spread on the topping. Cook until the bottom is slightly golden and the edges are crisp, about 3 to 5 minutes, depending on the heat source. Lightly spray the cooking surface with water between pies, and wipe away any debris.

   If you are using a conventional oven, preheat the oven to 400°F (200°C / Gas mark 6). Using the back of a spoon, spread the mixture over the prepared dough, leaving about ½in (1cm) of exposed dough at the edges. For more even distribution, use your fingertips. Bake for 7 to 10 minutes on the bottom shelf until the edges are slightly golden, watching carefully so they don't burn.

3. Serve the pies hot.

 Yields 4 pies.

☕ *Cook's Tip:* Another way to cook this pie is to fold the dough in half over the topping, forming a half-moon shape. This will prevent the cheese from drying out. Using a pastry brush, coat the pie with oil before cooking. Flip the pie over halfway through cooking. If you are using a conventional oven, you can sprinkle the dough with sesame seeds before cooking (they tend to burn on a griddle or convex disc). You can also make bite-sized Whey Cheese Pies by dividing the dough and filling into 16–20 equal pieces. If making bite-sized pies, bake on a lightly-oiled baking tray for 15 to 20 minutes.

Dried Yogurt & Bulgar

الكشك

Kishk

Kishk Pie

Dried Yogurt and Bulgar (*Kishk*)

Spicy Kishk Pie

Kishk Pie with Yogurt

Kishk Pie with Cheese

Kishk Pie with Vegetables

Kishk Pie with Walnuts

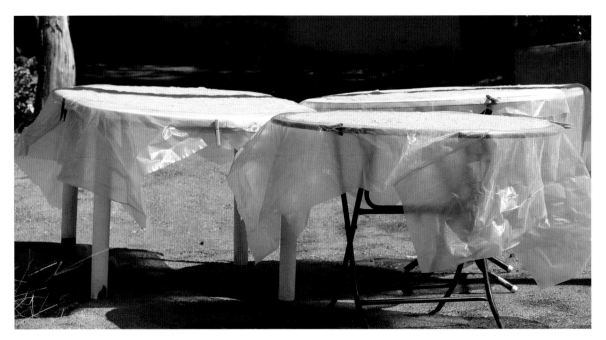

▶ *Kishk* drying in the sun.

▶ Antoinette Khalifeh teaching me to make *kishk*.

Kishk Pie

كشك

Kishk

Kishk is a fine powder made from a mixture of bulgar (cracked wheat, *burghul*) and yogurt, which has been carefully fermented. It is an important part of winter conservation in Lebanon. It is usually prepared in the beginning of October, when the weather is mild and sunny, and kept for year-round use. The actual procedure takes about a week and a half. In remote villages, you can see rooftops covered with white sheets, overlaid with *kishk*. Two patient women, Antoinette and Mounira, from the Khalifeh family in Ballouneh, took great pains to teach me exactly how to make *kishk*. Basically, the procedure is to mix yogurt (*laban*) with bulgar and salt. The mixture is fermented until sour, then it is dried it in the sun for three days, and crumbled periodically. This mixture is rubbed to a very fine powder and stored in airtight containers. Make your own, using the recipe on p. 97.

Prepare the dough on page 42.

1 dough recipe (see p. 42)

½ cup (2oz / 60g) of *kishk* (see p. 97)

2 medium tomatoes, finely chopped

1 medium onion, finely chopped or grated

1 teaspoon of tomato paste

½ cup (120ml) of olive oil

4 tablespoons of raw sesame seeds (optional)

1. In a bowl, mix the *kishk* with the tomatoes, onion, tomato paste, and olive oil. You may need to add some water to loosen the mixture to a sauce-like consistency.

2. If you are using a cast-iron crepe pan, griddle, or convex disc (*saj*), preheat over high heat. Heat the dough until small bubbles form; then lower the heat and spread on the topping and top with sesame seeds, if using. Cook until the bottom is slightly golden and the edges are crisp, about 3 to 5 minutes, depending on the heat source. Lightly spray the cooking surface with water between pies, and wipe away any debris.

   If you are using a conventional oven, preheat the oven to 400°F (200°C / Gas mark 6). Using the back of a spoon, spread the mixture over the prepared dough, leaving about ½in (1cm) of exposed dough at the edges. Top with sesame seeds, if using. Bake for 7 to 10 minutes on the bottom shelf until the edges are slightly golden, watching carefully so they don't burn.

3. Serve the pies hot.

 Yields 4 pies.

🍳 *Cook's Tip:* If preferred, you can sauté the onions and tomatoes separately in a small pan and then add the mixture to the *kishk* with the olive oil.

Dried Yogurt and Bulgar

Kishk

Kishk is a typical village staple, often served as a soup, cooked with meat preserve (*awarma*, see p.138), or seasoned with fried onions and garlic. It is made with white or brown wheat and goat's or cow's milk yogurt; sometimes sheep's milk is added, when available. In Lebanon, *kishk* production varies from one region to another. The most famous region known for *kishk* production is Baalbek, in the Beqa' Valley. Regional variations include the type of wheat and milk used, and the different techniques for making it. But collective secrets to producing good *kishk* are as follows: determining the exact amount of time needed for fermentation, watching for undesirable weather conditions, kneading the mixture thoroughly every day, and storing it properly to extend its shelf life.

2¼lb (1kg) of coarse white bulgar (cracked wheat, *burghul*)

17½lb (8kg) of plain yogurt

½ cup (5oz / 150g) coarse sea salt, ground

1. Wash the bulgar, spread on a tray, and leave it to dry in the sun (or a warm, dry place) for a few days.

2. While it's still warm from the sun, pour 4½lb (2kg) of the yogurt over the bulgar; cover with a thin cloth, and leave to rest overnight.

3. Next, strain the remaining yogurt to make *labneh*: Pour the remaining yogurt into a large bowl lined with a double layer of sterilized cheesecloth (muslin), leaving plenty of excess fabric to overlap the sides. Add about a third of the salt and mix thoroughly. Tie the ends of the cloth together over the yogurt and secure with a string. Hang it over the sink or a bowl in the refrigerator to drain overnight or until the contents are firm. You may need to drain for up to 2 days. Once firm, the curds should easily break away from the cloth.

4. The next day, pull away a third of the strained yogurt (*labneh*), leaving the rest to drain. In an earthenware basin, mix the strained yogurt you pulled out with a third of the salt and the bulgar. Mix again twice over the course of the day.

5. The next day, pull away half of the remaining strained yogurt, leaving the rest to drain. Add it to the mixture, again thoroughly mixing the ingredients together with your hands twice over the course of the day.

6. The next day, repeat the process with the remaining yogurt, adding the rest of the salt. Leave to ferment for 5 to 7 days, depending on weather conditions, mixing the ingredients thoroughly on a daily basis.

7. Spread lumps of the fermented mixture on a clean tray lined with a sterilized piece of cheesecloth (muslin). Leave to dry in the sun for 3 to 5 days.

8. Rub the lumps between the palms of your hands until they separate and form a coarse powder.

9. You can take this to your local mill to have it ground into a fine powder or grind it yourself by rubbing it through a sifter.

10. Leave the fine powder in the sun for 1 to 2 days to ensure complete dryness, as any humidly can spoil the *kishk*.

11. Store in an airtight container in a cool, dry place away from light. If stored properly, the *kishk* should keep for 12 to 18 months.

Yields approximately 6½lb (3kg)

◀ Tiny bite-sized *kishk* pies at a fancy reception in Beirut.

Spicy Kishk Pie

Kishk wa harr

كشك و حرّ

Kishk with a twist!

Prepare the dough on page 42.

1 dough recipe (see p.42)

½ cup (2oz / 60g) of *kishk* (see p. 97)

2 medium tomatoes, finely chopped

1 medium onion, finely chopped or grated

1 teaspoon of red pepper paste (see p. 153)

½ cup (120ml) of olive oil

4 tablespoons of raw sesame seeds (optional)

1. In a bowl, mix the *kishk* with the tomatoes, onion, red pepper paste, and olive oil. You may need to add some water to loosen the mixture to a sauce-like consistency.

2. If you are using a cast-iron crepe pan, griddle, or convex disc (*saj*), preheat over high heat. Heat the dough until small bubbles form; then lower the heat and spread on the topping and sprinkle with sesame seeds, if using. Cook until the bottom is slightly golden and the edges are crisp, about 3 to 5 minutes, depending on the heat source. Lightly spray the cooking surface with water between pies, and wipe away any debris.

   If you are using a conventional oven, preheat the oven to 400°F (200°C / Gas mark 6). Using the back of a spoon, spread the mixture over the prepared dough, leaving about ½in (1cm) of exposed dough at the edges, and sprinkle with sesame seeds, if using. Bake for 7 to 10 minutes on the bottom shelf until the edges are slightly golden, watching carefully so they don't burn.

3. Serve the pies hot.

 Yields 4 pies.

 Cook's Tip: If preferred, you can sauté the onions and tomatoes separately in a small pan before adding to the mixture.

▶ A busy bakery in the souk of Baalbek.

Kishk Pie with Yogurt

Kishk wa laban

Adding fresh yogurt to the *kishk* gives the pie a lighter texture.

Prepare the dough on page 42.

1 dough recipe (see p. 42)

½ cup (2oz / 60g) of *kishk* (see p. 97)

1 medium onion, finely chopped

½ cup (120ml) of plain yogurt (or more, if needed)

½ cup (120ml) of olive oil

4 tablespoons of raw sesame seeds (optional)

1. In a bowl, mix the *kishk* with the onion, yogurt, and olive oil. You may need to add more yogurt to loosen the mixture to a sauce-like consistency.

2. If you are using a cast-iron crepe pan, griddle, or convex disc (*saj*), preheat over high heat. Heat the dough until small bubbles form. Lower the heat, spread on the topping, and sprinkle with sesame seeds, if using. Cook until the bottom is slightly golden and the edges are crisp, about 3 to 5 minutes, depending on the heat source. Lightly spray the cooking surface with water between pies, and wipe away any debris.

   If you are using a conventional oven, preheat the oven to 400°F (200°C / Gas mark 6). Using the back of a spoon, spread the mixture over the prepared dough, leaving about ½in (1cm) around the edges, and sprinkle with sesame seeds, if using. Bake for 7 to 10 minutes on the bottom shelf until the edges are slightly golden, watching carefully so they don't burn.

3. Serve the pies hot.

 Yields 4 pies.

Kishk Pie with Cheese

Kishk wa jibneh

This recipe is not very common, but worth trying.

Prepare the dough on page 42.

1 dough recipe (see p. 42)

½ cup (2oz / 60g) of *kishk* (see p. 97)

1 cup (4oz / 120g) of *'akkawi* cheese

2 medium onions, finely chopped

½ cup (120ml) of olive oil

4 tablespoons of raw sesame seeds (optional)

1. *'Akkawi* cheese is very salty. To reduce the salt content, soak the grated cheese in water overnight. Change the water two or three times, if possible. If time does not permit, soak the grated cheese for a couple of hours, then run cold water over the cheese in a colander. Drain well before using.

2. In a bowl, mix the *kishk* with the *'akkawi* cheese, onions, and olive oil. You may need to add some water to loosen the mixture to a sauce-like consistency.

3. If you are using a cast-iron crepe pan, griddle, or convex disc (*saj*), preheat over high heat. Heat the dough until small bubbles form. Lower the heat, spread on the topping, and sprinkle with sesame seeds, if using. Cook until the bottom is slightly golden and the edges are crisp, about 3 to 5 minutes, depending on the heat source. Lightly spray the cooking surface with water between pies, and wipe away any debris.

   If you are using a conventional oven, preheat the oven to 400°F (200°C / Gas mark 6). Using the back of a spoon, spread the mixture over the prepared dough, leaving about ½in (1cm) around the edges, and sprinkle with sesame seeds, if using. Bake for 7 to 10 minutes on the bottom shelf until the edges are slightly golden, watching carefully so they don't burn.

4. Serve the pies hot.

◄ Traditional handmade pottery used in the process of making yogurt (*laban*).

 Yields 4 pies.

► This delightful woman makes a very tasty *kishk* pie. I always stop by her bakery on my way to Ramlieh, a charming village in the Shouf.

Kishk Pie with Vegetables

Kishk wa khodra

كشك وخضرة

The green bell pepper adds an extra element to this flavorful topping.

1 dough recipe (see p. 42)

½ cup (2oz / 60g) of *kishk* (see p. 97)

2 medium tomatoes, finely chopped

1 medium onion, finely chopped

½ to 1 medium green bell pepper, finely chopped

½ cup (120ml) of olive oil

Prepare the dough on page 42.

1. In a bowl, mix the *kishk* with the tomatoes, onion, green pepper, and olive oil. You may need to add some water to loosen the mixture to obtain a sauce-like consistency.

2. If you are using a cast-iron crepe pan, griddle, or convex disc (*saj*), preheat over high heat. Heat the dough until small bubbles form. Lower the heat and spread on the topping. Cook until the bottom is slightly golden and the edges are crisp, about 3 to 5 minutes, depending on the heat source. Lightly spray the cooking surface with water between pies, and wipe away any debris.

   If you are using a conventional oven, preheat the oven to 400°F (200°C / Gas mark 6). Using the back of a spoon, spread the mixture over the prepared dough, leaving about ½in (1cm) around the edges. Bake for 7 to 10 minutes on the bottom shelf until the edges are slightly golden, watching carefully so they don't burn.

3. Serve the pies hot.

 Yields 4 pies.

Kishk Pie with Walnuts

Kishk wa jawz

كشك وجوز

I learned to make this recipe one day while working in the bakery next to my house. Laudy Gebrael came into the bakery with this topping. She shared her recipe with me and offered me one of her pies. It was truly extraordinary!

Prepare the dough on page 42.

1 dough recipe (see p. 42)

½ cup (2oz / 60g) of *kishk* (see p. 97)

2 medium tomatoes, finely chopped

1 medium onion, finely chopped

½ cup of finely-chopped walnuts

1 teaspoon of tomato paste

1 teaspoon to 1 tablespoon of red pepper paste (see p. 153)

½ cup (120ml) of olive oil

4 tablespoons of raw sesame seeds (optional)

1. In a bowl, mix the *kishk* with the tomatoes, onion, nuts, tomato paste, red pepper paste, and olive oil. You may need to add some water to loosen the mixture to a sauce-like consistency.

2. If you are using a cast-iron crepe pan, griddle, or convex disc (*saj*), preheat over high heat. Heat the dough until small bubbles form. Lower the heat, spread on the topping, and sprinkle with sesame seeds, if using. Cook until the bottom is slightly golden and the edges are crisp, about 3 to 5 minutes, depending on the heat source. Lightly spray the cooking surface with water between pies, and wipe away any debris.

   If you are using a conventional oven, preheat the oven to 400°F (200°C / Gas mark 6). Using the back of a spoon, spread the mixture over the prepared dough, leaving about ½in (1cm) around the edges, and sprinkle with sesame seeds, if using. Bake for 7 to 10 minutes on the bottom shelf until the edges are slightly golden, watching carefully so they don't burn.

3. Serve the pies hot.

 Yields 4 pies.

Cook's Tip: If the *kishk* is made with cow's milk, you can add 1 tablespoon of lemon juice to give it a tangier flavor.

الفطائر **Turnovers**
Fatayer

Spinach Turnovers

Zucchini Turnovers

Swiss Chard Turnovers

Purslane Turnovers

Spinach Turnovers

قطائر بالسبانخ

Fatayer bi-sbanekh

A turnover can be a light meal in itself, or it can be served as part of a *mezze* spread.

Prepare the dough on page 42, dividing the dough into 4–6 equal pieces for large turnovers, or 16–20 pieces if making bite-sized turnovers (you can roll the dough out and cut out the pieces using a cookie cutter or glass). If making bite-sized turnovers, add ¼ cup (60ml) of vegetable oil to the dough recipe and bake in the oven for 15 to 20 minutes.

1 modified dough recipe (see p. 42)

4lb (2kg) bunch of spinach, leaves pulled away from the stalk (or 1lb / 450g spinach leaves)

1 tablespoon of salt

1 medium onion, finely chopped

1 medium tomato, finely chopped

3 to 4 tablespoons of ground sumac

Juice of 1 lemon

1 cup (250ml) of olive oil

1 tablespoon of vegetable oil

1. Wash the spinach leaves carefully; you may need to do this several times. Drain well, drying the leaves as much as possible. Coarsely chop the leaves.

2. Add the salt and gently rub the salt and spinach together. This will help draw out any excess water. Drain the spinach again.

3. In a large bowl, combine the spinach, onion, tomato, sumac, lemon juice, and olive oil. Mix well with your hands, squeezing out any excess liquid. If your hands are sensitive to lemon juice, wear gloves.

4. Divide the filling according to how many turnovers you are making (a generous tablespoonful each for small pies, and about a cup for larger pies).

5. Place a portion of the filling in the center of a dough circle. Fold the dough over the filling in thirds, pinching the edges together so you have a triangular parcel (see photo on p. 108). Repeat until all the dough circles have been filled.

6. Using a pastry brush, coat the turnovers with vegetable oil and let them stand for half an hour before baking.

7. If you are using a cast-iron crepe pan, griddle, or convex disc, preheat over medium heat. Lower the heat and place turnovers on the surface. Cook until the bottoms are slightly golden and the edges are crisp, about 5 to 7 minutes, turning over halfway through. Lightly spray the cooking surface with water between batches, and wipe away any debris.

   If you are using a conventional oven, place turnovers on a lightly-oiled baking tray and preheat the oven to 400°F (200°C / Gas mark 6). Bake for 7 to 10 minutes on the bottom shelf until the edges are slightly golden, watching carefully so they don't burn.

8. The turnovers can be served hot or at room temperature.

△ *Yields 4–6 large or 16–20 bite-sized turnovers.*

🍲 *Cook's Tip:* You can add ½ cup (2oz / 50g) of crushed walnuts, raisins, or pine nuts to the mixture. You can also add cheese for more flavor: ½ cup (2½oz / 75g) of a mixture of *'akkawi* cheese and feta cheese is tastiest.

▶ Naïm Hayek making bite-sized turnovers at Trés Bon Bakery in Chiyah.

Zucchini Turnovers

Fatayer bi-coussa

قطائر بكوسا

This turnover is not common in bakeries, but is becoming more popular in Lebanese households. Many families make their own filling and take it to the bakery. If you love zucchini, you're in for a treat!

Prepare the dough on page 42, dividing the dough into 4–6 equal pieces for large turnovers, or 16–20 pieces if making bite-sized turnovers (you can roll the dough out and cut out the pieces using a cookie cutter or glass). If making bite-sized turnovers, add ¼ cup (60ml) of vegetable oil to the dough recipe and bake in the oven for 15 to 20 minutes.

1 modified dough recipe (see p. 42)

3–4 cups (1lb / 500g) of grated zucchini

1 medium onion, finely chopped

1 medium tomato, finely chopped

1 tablespoon of ground sumac

1 teaspoon of salt

½ teaspoon of black or red pepper

Juice of 1 lemon

½ cup (120ml) of olive oil

1 tablespoon of vegetable oil

1. Drain the grated zucchini in a colander, squeezing out as much liquid as possible.

2. In a large bowl, combine the zucchini, onion, tomato, sumac, salt, pepper, lemon juice, and olive oil. Mix well, using your hands. If your hands are sensitive to lemon juice, wear gloves. Drain the mixture again to remove any excess liquid.

3. Divide the filling according to how many turnovers you are making (a generous tablespoonful each for small pies, and about a cup for larger pies).

4. Place a portion of the filling in the center of a dough circle. Fold the dough over the filling in thirds, pinching the edges together so you have a triangular parcel (see photo on p. 107). Repeat until all the dough circles have been filled.

5. Using a pastry brush, coat the turnovers with vegetable oil and let stand for half an hour before baking.

6. If you are using a cast-iron crepe pan, griddle, or convex disc, preheat over medium heat. Lower the heat and place turnovers on the surface. Cook until the bottoms are slightly golden and the edges are crisp, about 5 to 7 minutes, turning over halfway through. Lightly spray the cooking surface with water between batches, and wipe away any debris.

   If you are using a conventional oven, place turnovers on a lightly-oiled baking tray and preheat the oven to 400°F (200°C / Gas mark 6). Bake for 7 to 10 minutes on the bottom shelf until the edges are slightly golden, watching carefully so they don't burn.

7. The turnovers can be served hot or at room temperature.

△ *Yields 4–6 large or 16–20 bite-sized turnovers.*

🎩 *Cook's Tip:* You can add ½ cup (2oz / 50g) of crushed walnuts, raisins, or pine nuts to the mixture. Alternatively, add chopped boiled potatoes and a dash of curry powder or cumin for an exotic flavor.

Swiss Chard Turnovers

Fatayer bi-sele'

فطاير بسلق

The most popular turnovers in the bakeries are the ones made with spinach or Swiss chard.

Prepare the dough on page 42, dividing the dough into 4–6 equal pieces for large turnovers, or 16–20 pieces if making bite-sized turnovers (you can roll the dough out and cut out the pieces using a cookie cutter or glass). If making bite-sized turnovers, add ¼ cup (60ml) of vegetable oil to the dough recipe and bake in the oven for 15 to 20 minutes.

1 modified dough recipe (see p. 42)

4lb (2kg) bunch of Swiss chard, leaves and tender stems coarsely chopped

1 medium onion, finely chopped

1 medium tomato, finely chopped

2 tablespoons of ground sumac

Juice of 1 lemon

1 teaspoon of salt

½ cup (120ml) of olive oil

1 tablespoon of vegetable oil

1. Carefully wash and dry the Swiss chard.

2. In a large bowl, combine the Swiss chard, onion, tomato, sumac, lemon juice, salt, and olive oil. Mix well using your hands and squeeze out any excess water. If your hands are sensitive to lemon juice, wear gloves. Drain well.

3. Divide the filling according to how many turnovers you are making (a generous tablespoon each for small pies, and about a cup for larger pies).

4. Place a portion of the filling in the center of a dough circle. Fold the dough over the filling in thirds, pinching the edges together so you have a triangular parcel (see photos on p. 108 and 111). Repeat until all the dough circles have been filled.

5. Using a pastry brush, coat the turnovers with vegetable oil and let stand for half an hour before baking.

6. If you are using a cast-iron crepe pan, griddle, or convex disc, preheat over medium heat. Lower the heat and place turnovers on the surface. Cook until the bottoms are slightly golden and the edges are crisp, about 5 to 7 minutes, turning over halfway through. Lightly spray the cooking surface with water between batches, and wipe away any debris.

   If you are using a conventional oven, place turnovers on a lightly-oiled baking tray and preheat the oven to 400°F (200°C / Gas mark 6). Bake for 7 to 10 minutes on the bottom shelf until the edges are slightly golden, watching carefully so they don't burn.

7. The turnovers can be served hot or at room temperature.

△ *Yields 4–6 large or 16–20 bite-sized turnovers.*

☕ *Cook's Tip:* You can add ½ cup (2oz / 50g) of crushed walnuts, raisins, or pine nuts to the mixture.

Purslane Turnovers

Fatayer bi-baqleh

فطاير بالبقلة

Purslane is a commonly used green in Lebanon. The leaves of the purslane plant are also used in the famous peasant salad, *fattoush*. Its sharp taste blends well with onions and tomatoes.

Prepare the dough on page 42, dividing the dough into 4–6 equal pieces for large turnovers, or 16–20 pieces if making bite-sized turnovers (you can roll the dough out and cut out the pieces using a cookie cutter or glass). If making bite-sized turnovers, add ¼ cup (60ml) of vegetable oil to the dough recipe and bake in the oven for 15 to 20 minutes.

1 modified dough recipe (see p. 42)

4 bunches (about 2 cups) of purslane leaves

1 medium onion, finely chopped

2 medium tomatoes, finely chopped

1–2 tablespoons of ground sumac

Juice of 1 lemon

1 tablespoon of salt

½ cup (120ml) of olive oil

1 tablespoon of vegetable oil

1. Thoroughly wash and dry the purslane leaves.

2. In a large bowl, combine the purslane, onion, tomatoes, ground sumac, lemon juice, salt, and olive oil. Mix well using your hands and squeeze out any excess water. If your hands are sensitive to lemon juice, wear gloves. Drain well.

3. Divide the filling according to how many turnovers you are making (a generous tablespoon each for small pies, and about a cup for larger pies).

4. Place a portion of the filling in the center of a dough circle. Fold the dough over the filling in thirds, pinching the edges together so you have a triangular parcel (see photos on p. 108 and 111). Repeat until all the dough circles have been filled.

5. Using a pastry brush, coat the turnovers with vegetable oil and let stand for half an hour before baking.

6. If you are using a cast-iron crepe pan, griddle, or convex disc, preheat over medium heat. Lower the heat and place turnovers on the surface. Cook until the bottoms are slightly golden and the edges are crisp, about 5 to 7 minutes, turning over halfway through. Lightly spray the cooking surface with water between batches, and wipe away any debris.

   If you are using a conventional oven, place turnovers on a lightly-oiled baking tray and preheat the oven to 400°F (200°C / Gas mark 6). Bake for 7 to 10 minutes on the bottom shelf until the edges are slightly golden, watching carefully so they don't burn.

7. The turnovers can be served hot or at room temperature.

△ *Yields 4–6 large or 16–20 bite-sized turnovers.*

🍳 *Cook's Tip:* You can replace the purslane leaves with wild thyme, lettuce, or any wild greens like dandelion greens, wild chicory, or sorrel.

Vegetarian

نباتي

Nabati

Vegetarian Pie

Spicy Red Pepper Pie

Tomato Pie

Mushroom Pie

Fresh Thyme Pie

Chickpea Pie

كزّبة Vegetarian Pie

Kezzebeh

This pie is referred to as *kezzebeh*, meaning liar in Arabic. During the Christian Lent period, many bakeries don't bake meat pies. Also, in times of war, meat was sometimes scarce or expensive. It was then that the vegetarian pie became popular.

Prepare the dough on page 42.

1 dough recipe (see p. 42)

2 medium onions, finely chopped

4 medium tomatoes, finely chopped

1 medium green bell pepper, finely chopped

1 tablespoon of ground sumac

½ teaspoon of red pepper powder

½ cup (120ml) of olive oil

1 tablespoon of salt

4 tablespoons of raw sesame seeds (optional)

1. In a bowl, mix the onions, tomatoes, green bell pepper, sumac, red pepper powder, olive oil, and salt.

2. If you are using a cast-iron crepe pan, griddle, or convex disc (*saj*), preheat over high heat. Heat the dough until small bubbles form. Lower the heat, spread on the topping, and sprinkle with sesame seeds, if using. Cook until the bottom is slightly golden and the edges are crisp, about 3 to 5 minutes, depending on the heat source. Lightly spray the cooking surface with water between pies, and wipe away any debris.

If you are using a conventional oven, preheat the oven to 400°F (200°C / Gas mark 6). Using the back of a spoon, spread the mixture over the prepared dough, leaving about ½in (1cm) around the edges, and sprinkle with sesame seeds, if using. Bake for 7 to 10 minutes on the bottom shelf until the edges are slightly golden, watching carefully so they don't burn.

3. Serve the pies hot.

 Yields 4 pies.

▶ A handsome boy I found eating at *Zaatar w Zeit*, a fashionable restaurant, where you can enjoy a wide array of pies typical of street corner bakeries—morning, noon, and night!

Spicy Red Pepper Pie

Flayfleh harra

فلافل حرّة

This is definitely hot and spicy! It is a favorite among the Armenian community.

Prepare the dough on page 42.

1 dough recipe (see p. 42)

2 medium onions, finely chopped

¼ cup (60ml) of red pepper paste (see p. 153)

1 cup (8oz / 150g) of ground walnuts

1 cup (250ml) of olive oil

Pinch of cumin

1. In a bowl, mix the onions, red pepper paste, walnuts, olive oil, and cumin.

2. If you are using a cast-iron crepe pan, griddle, or convex disc (*saj*), preheat over high heat. Heat the dough until small bubbles form; then lower the heat and spread on the topping. Cook until the bottom is slightly golden and the edges are crisp, about 3 to 5 minutes, depending on the heat source. Lightly spray the cooking surface with water between pies, and wipe away any debris.

   If you are using a conventional oven, preheat the oven to 400°F (200°C / Gas mark 6). Using the back of a spoon, spread the mixture over the prepared dough, leaving about ½in (1cm) of exposed dough at the edges. For more even distribution, use your fingertips. Bake for 7 to 10 minutes on the bottom shelf until the edges are slightly golden, watching carefully so they don't burn.

3. Serve the pies hot.

Yields 4 pies.

 Cook's Tip: You can add 1 finely-chopped tomato to the mixture. You can also omit the walnuts and spread a layer of *'akkawi* cheese on top of the mixture.

◄ Selim el Sayegh, a farmer from Sofar village. A very memorable encounter.

نَدُورة **Tomato Pie**

Banadoura

For this recipe, use fresh, ripe tomatoes.

Prepare the dough on page 42.

1 dough recipe (see p. 42)

4 medium tomatoes, finely chopped

1 medium onion, finely chopped

1 teaspoon of salt

4 tablespoons of olive oil

Fresh thyme leaves, to garnish (optional)

1. In a mixing bowl, blend the tomatoes and the onions. Add salt. If tomatoes are too watery, drain in a colander.

2. If you are using a cast-iron crepe pan, griddle, or convex disc (*saj*), preheat over high heat. Heat the dough until small bubbles form; then lower the heat and spread on the topping. Cook until the bottom is slightly golden and the edges are crisp, about 3 to 5 minutes, depending on the heat source. Lightly spray the cooking surface with water between pies, and wipe away any debris.

   If you are using a conventional oven, preheat the oven to 400°F (200°C / Gas mark 6). Using the back of a spoon, spread the mixture over the prepared dough, leaving about ½in (1cm) of exposed dough at the edges. For more even distribution, use your fingertips. Bake for 7 to 10 minutes on the bottom shelf until the edges are slightly golden, watching carefully so they don't burn.

3. For extra flavor, drizzle 1 tablespoon of olive oil on each cooked pie.

4. Serve the pies hot. Top with fresh thyme leaves, if using.

 Yields 4 pies.

Mushroom Pie

Fitr

For those who love the taste of meat pies but for one reason or another do not eat meat, this is a perfect substitute. Mrs. Ichkhanian gave me this original recipe. I haven't seen it anywhere else!

Prepare the dough on page 42, omitting the oil and sugar. On a generously floured surface, divide dough into 16 equal pieces and roll out paper-thin (or roll the dough and cut out discs using a large cookie cutter or glass).

1 modified dough recipe (see p. 42)

4½ cups (1lb / 450g) of canned or fresh mushrooms

2 medium onions

½ green bell pepper

4 large or 6 medium tomatoes

1 small bunch of flat-leaf parsley, finely chopped

5 garlic cloves, minced

½ teaspoon of allspice

1½ teaspoons of salt

Pinch of black pepper

1. Wash the canned mushrooms under cold water and drain, or wipe the fresh mushrooms.

2. Finely chop the mushrooms, onions, green pepper, and tomatoes (or quarter them and pulse them in a food processor.)

3. Drain any excess liquid through a colander. Add the parsley, garlic, allspice, salt, and pepper to the vegetables and mix well.

4. Thinly spread the mixture over the whole surface of the dough.

5. If you are using a cast-iron crepe pan, griddle, or convex disc (*saj*), preheat over low heat. Cook the pies until the undersides are slightly golden and the edges are crisp, about 3 to 5 minutes, depending on the heat source. Lightly spray the cooking surface with water between batches and wipe away any debris.

   If you are using a conventional oven, preheat the oven to 400°F (200°C / Gas mark 6). Bake for 5 to 7 minutes on the bottom shelf until the edges are slightly golden, watching carefully so they don't burn.

6. Serve the pies hot or at room temperature.

Yields 16 pies.

Fresh Thyme Pie

Za'tar akhdar

Walking down the street one day in Barbir in Beirut, I saw a baker carrying a wooden board filled with delicious pies. One of his customers shared his wife's recipe.

Prepare the dough on page 42.

1 dough recipe (see p. 42)

2 medium tomatoes, finely chopped

1 large onion, finely chopped

2 small red or green hot peppers, very finely chopped

1 bunch of fresh thyme springs, chopped

1 cup (250ml) of lemon juice

½ cup (120ml) of olive oil

1 teaspoon of salt

½ teaspoon of black pepper

1. In a bowl, mix tomatoes, onion, hot peppers, thyme, lemon juice, olive oil, salt, and pepper.

2. If you are using a cast-iron crepe pan, griddle, or convex disc (*saj*), preheat over high heat. Heat the dough until small bubbles form; then lower the heat and spread on the topping. Cook until the bottom is slightly golden and the edges are crisp, about 3 to 5 minutes, depending on the heat source. Lightly spray the cooking surface with water between pies, and wipe away any debris.

   If you are using a conventional oven, preheat the oven to 400°F (200°C / Gas mark 6). Using the back of a spoon, spread the mixture over the prepared dough, leaving about ½in (1cm) of exposed dough at the edges. For more even distribution, use your fingertips. Bake for 7 to 10 minutes on the bottom shelf until the edges are slightly golden, watching carefully so they don't burn.

3. Serve the pies hot.

 Yields 4 pies.

Cook's Tip: You can also use this recipe to make turnovers (follow the procedure on p. 111).

◀ This pie reminds me of the Italian *focaccia*.

Chickpea Pie

Hboub hommos

An innovative way to eat chickpeas!

Prepare the dough on page 42.

1 dough recipe (see p. 42)

1¾ cups (½lb / 250g) of dried chickpeas, soaked overnight in water and 1 teaspoon of baking soda (or 1 can of cooked chickpeas)

2 garlic cloves, crushed

½ cup (120ml) of olive oil

1. Drain the chickpeas and simmer on low heat in fresh water until tender, about 15 to 30 minutes. (If using canned chickpeas, omit this step.) Drain.

2. In a bowl, combine the chickpeas with the crushed garlic and olive oil and mix well, until the chickpeas are well coated.

3. Spread chickpeas onto the prepared dough. Pass the rolling pin over the chickpeas until they stick firmly in the dough.

4. If you are using a cast-iron crepe pan, griddle, or convex disc (*saj*), preheat over high heat. Cook the pies until the bottom is slightly golden and the edges are crisp, about 3 to 5 minutes, depending on the heat source. Lightly spray the cooking surface with water between pies, and wipe away any debris.

   If you are using a conventional oven, preheat the oven to 400°F (200°C / Gas mark 6). Bake for 7 to 10 minutes on the bottom shelf until the edges are slightly golden, watching carefully so they don't burn.

5. Serve the pies hot, accompanied by an assortment of fresh vegetables and dips.

 Yields 4 pies.

► Young boys in the souk of Saida carrying a bunch of fresh green chickpeas.

Egg
البيض *Bayd*

Egg Pie

Egg Pie with Cheese

Egg Pie with Vegetables

 **Egg Pie**
Bayd

This recipe is popular in the villages of Batroun, in the north of Lebanon.

Prepare the dough on page 42.

1 dough recipe (see p. 42)

8 large eggs (2 eggs for each pie), at room temperature

1 teaspoon of salt

½ teaspoon of black pepper

1. Break the eggs into a mixing bowl and beat well. Add salt and pepper.

2. Using your fingertips, raise the edges of the dough slightly to prevent the eggs from running.

3. If you are using a cast-iron crepe pan, griddle, or convex disc (*saj*), preheat over high heat. Heat the dough until small bubbles form; then lower the heat and very carefully pour in the eggs. Cook until the eggs have set and the edges are crisp, about 3 to 5 minutes, depending on the heat source. Lightly spray the cooking surface with water between pies, and wipe away any debris.

   If you are using a conventional oven, preheat the oven to 400°F (200°C / Gas mark 6). Carefully pour in the eggs and bake the pies for 7 to 10 minutes on the bottom shelf until the eggs are cooked and the edges are slightly golden, watching carefully so they don't burn.

4. Serve the pies hot, accompanied by an assortment of fresh vegetables.

 Yields 4 pies.

▶ Baking has no age: a 90-year-old woman from Douma selling *man'oushé* at the Souk el Tayeb annual festival.

Egg Pie with Cheese

Bayd wa jibneh

A delicious omelette served on crusty dough!

Prepare the dough on page 42.

1 dough recipe (see p. 42)

8 large eggs (2 for each pie), at room temperature

3½ cups (8oz / 225g) of grated cheese (mozzarella, white cheddar, or *shankleesh*, see p. 77)

1 teaspoon of salt

½ teaspoon of black pepper

1. Break the eggs into a mixing bowl and beat well. Add cheese, salt, and pepper, and mix.

2. Using your fingertips, raise the edges of the dough slightly to prevent the eggs from running.

3. If you are using a cast-iron crepe pan, griddle, or convex disc (*saj*), preheat over high heat. Heat the dough until small bubbles form; then lower the heat and very carefully pour in the egg mixture. Cook until the eggs have set and the edges are crisp, about 3 to 5 minutes, depending on the heat source. Lightly spray the cooking surface with water between pies, and wipe away any debris.

   If you are using a conventional oven, preheat the oven to 400°F (200°C / Gas mark 6). Carefully pour in the egg mixture and bake the pies for 7 to 10 minutes on the bottom shelf until the eggs are cooked and the edges are slightly golden, watching carefully so they don't burn.

4. Serve the pies hot.

 Yields 4 pies.

Egg Pie with Vegetables

Bayd wa khodra

This pie is a meal in itself! It reminds me of lazy mornings with my family.

Prepare the dough on page 42.

1 dough recipe (see p. 42)

8 large eggs (2 for each pie), at room temperature

1 medium onion, finely chopped

2 medium tomatoes, finely chopped

1 bunch of fresh mint leaves, finely chopped

½ bunch of fresh flat-leaf parsley, finely chopped

1 teaspoon salt

½ teaspoon of black pepper

Pinch of cinnamon

1 tablespoon of vegetable oil

1. In a mixing bowl, beat the eggs. Add the onion, tomatoes, mint, parsley, salt, pepper, cinnamon, and vegetable oil, and mix well.

2. Using your fingertips, raise the edges of the dough slightly to prevent the eggs from running.

3. If you are using a cast-iron crepe pan, griddle, or convex disc (*saj*), preheat over high heat. Heat the dough until small bubbles form; then lower the heat and very carefully ladle in the egg mixture. Cook until the eggs have set and the edges are crisp, about 3 to 5 minutes, depending on the heat source. Lightly spray the cooking surface with water between pies, and wipe away any debris.

   If you are using a conventional oven, preheat the oven to 400°F (200°C / Gas mark 6). Carefully ladle in the egg mixture and bake the pies for 7 to 10 minutes on the bottom shelf until the eggs are cooked and the edges are slightly golden, watching carefully so they don't burn.

4. Serve the pies hot.

 Yields 4 pies.

◀ A couple wearing traditional dress.

 Cook's Tip: You can replace the mint leaves with half of a green bell pepper, finely chopped.

Chicken

الدجاج

Djeij

Chicken Pie

Chicken Pie with Cilantro
and Garlic

Chicken Pie

Djeij

You will not find this pie at the local bakery. The mixture is adapted from a recipe at the bakery of the famous Phoenicia Hotel in the center of Beirut.

Start with the dough on page 42, omitting the oil and sugar.
Divide dough into 10 equal pieces and roll out very thinly.

1 modified dough recipe (see p. 42)

1 medium onion

5 garlic cloves

1½ teaspoons of salt

1lb (500g) of finely-ground chicken

½ cup (120ml) of olive oil

1 tablespoon of tomato paste

Juice of 2 lemons

½ teaspoon of cumin (optional)

Pinch of white pepper

4 lemon wedges

1. Finely chop the onion, or pulse in a food processor.

2. Using a mortar and pestle, crush the garlic cloves with ½ teaspoon of salt.

3. In a bowl, combine the ground chicken with the oil, tomato paste, lemon juice, cumin (if using), pepper, and the remaining salt. Add the onions and the garlic mixture and mix well, kneading to create a dough-like consistency.

4. Divide the mixture into 10 parts. This can be done easily with a sharp dough scraper. Thinly spread the mixture over the whole surface of the dough; the chicken will shrink while cooking.

5. If you are using a cast-iron crepe pan, griddle, or convex disc (*saj*), preheat over low heat. This is important so the chicken cooks evenly. Cook until the chicken is cooked and the bottoms are slightly golden, about 5 minutes, depending on the heat source. Lightly spray the cooking surface with water between batches, and wipe away any debris.

   If you are using a conventional oven, preheat the oven to 400°F (200°C / Gas mark 6). Bake for 5 to 7 minutes on the bottom shelf until the chicken is cooked and the bottoms are slightly golden, watching carefully so they don't burn.

6. Serve the pies hot with lemon wedges, since the chicken may dry out a little as it cooks.

Yields 10 pies.

 Cook's Tip: You can add ½ bunch of flat-leaf parsley, finely chopped, to the mixture.

► Mona and Nelly preparing paper-thin bread for the weekly farmer's market.

Chicken Pie with Cilantro and Garlic

جاج بكزبرة وثوم

Djeij bi kizbara wa toum

The flavor of this pie is reminiscent of the famous *shish taouk*, a staple of Lebanese cuisine. *Shish taouk* is grilled, cubed chicken breast that has been marinated in a garlic sauce.

Prepare the dough on page 42, omitting the oil and sugar.
Divide dough into 10 equal pieces and roll out very thinly.

1 modified dough recipe (see p. 42)

1 leek

5 garlic cloves

1½ teaspoons of salt

½ cup (120ml) of olive oil

1 bunch of fresh cilantro (coriander)

1lb (450g) of finely-ground chicken

Pinch of white pepper

Juice of 1 lemon

4 lemon wedges, to garnish

1. Wash and finely chop the leek.

2. Using a mortar and pestle, crush the garlic cloves with ½ teaspoon of salt. Fry the garlic in olive oil with the cilantro.

3. In a bowl, mix the chicken with the pepper, lemon juice, and the remaining salt. Add the leek and the garlic mixture and mix well, kneading to create a dough-like consistency.

4. Divide the mixture into 10 parts. This can be done easily with a sharp dough scraper. Thinly spread the mixture over the whole surface of the dough; the chicken will shrink while cooking.

5. If you are using a cast-iron crepe pan, griddle, or convex disc (*saj*), preheat over low heat. This is important to make sure that the chicken cooks evenly. Cook until the chicken is cooked and the bottoms are slightly golden, about 5 minutes, depending on the heat source. Lightly spray the cooking surface with water between batches, and wipe away any debris.

   If you are using a conventional oven, preheat the oven to 400°F (200°C / Gas mark 6). Bake for 5 to 7 minutes on the bottom shelf until the chicken is cooked and the bottoms are slightly golden, watching carefully so they don't burn.

6. Serve the pies hot with lemon wedges, since the chicken may dry out a little as it cooks.

 Yields 10 pies.

◄ Garlic hanging to dry.

Meat Preserve

الأورما

Awarma

Meat Preserve Pie

Meat Preserve Pie with Eggs

Meat Preserve Pie with Strained Yogurt

Meat Preserve Pie with Kishk

Meat Preserve Pie with Hummus

Meat Preserve Pie

فوارما

Awarma

Awarma is an important aspect of mountain life. This preserve was traditionally made when a sheep was slain in the center of a village, to sustain the villagers through the winter. It is quite tasty, but I warn you, it is on the heavier side. This recipe can be halved or quartered.

FOR THE MEAT PRESERVE (*AWARMA*)

4 cups (2lb / 1kg) of mutton fat (suet), roughly chopped

2 cups (1lb / ½ kg) of lean, finely-ground lamb (or lamb cubes)

2½ teaspoons of coarse sea salt

🍶 Makes a half-gallon (2kg) jar (about 8 cups)

FOR THE PIE

1 dough recipe (see p. 42)

2 cups (14oz / 400g) of meat preserve (*awarma*), approximately ½ cup for each pie

FOR THE MEAT PRESERVE (*AWARMA*)

1. Pour ½ cup of water into a large Dutch oven. This will keep the fat from sticking to the surface of the pot. Add the fat and cook over medium heat until it has completely melted.

2. Next, add the meat and the salt. Cook, stirring constantly to break up the pieces, until the meat has cooked thoroughly and evenly, about 30 to 45 minutes.

3. Cool the mixture fully and store in a sterilized jar in the refrigerator. If properly stored, *awarma* can keep for several months.

🍳 *Cook's Tip:* When cooking the meat preserve, you can add a whole peeled onion to the pot; this helps reduce scum and adds a light flavor to the cooked meat (remove before storing). You can also add allspice and cinnamon to the meat before cooking, if desired.

FOR THE PIE

Prepare the dough on page 42.

1. If you are using a cast-iron crepe pan, griddle, or convex disc (*saj*), preheat over high heat. Heat the dough until small bubbles form; then lower the heat and melt the meat preserve in the middle of the dough for about 30 seconds, before spreading it evenly on the dough. This method will prevent fat from running onto the cooking surface. Cook until the bottom is slightly golden and the edges are crisp, about 3 to 5 minutes, depending on the heat source. Lightly spray the cooking surface with water between pies, and wipe away any debris.

   If you are using a conventional oven, preheat the oven to 400°F (200°C / Gas mark 6). Spread the meat preserve carefully on the prepared dough, leaving about ½in (1cm) of exposed dough at the edges. Bake for 7 to 10 minutes on the bottom shelf until the dough is slightly golden, watching carefully to make sure it does not burn.

2. Serve the pies hot.

🍞 *Yields 4 pies.*

▶ A hungry Beirut taxi driver stops for a snack.

◄ Traditionally handcrafted pottery in the village of Assia in Batroun.

Meat Preserve Pie with Eggs

قورمة وبيض

Awarma wa bayd

Whenever I mention this pie to people in Lebanon, I always get a smile. Is it perhaps that it brings back childhood memories?

1 dough recipe (see p. 42)

8 large eggs (2 for each pie) at room temperature

2 cups (14oz / 400g) of meat preserve (*awarma*, see p.138), approximately ½ cup for each pie

1 teaspoon of allspice

Salt, to taste

Prepare the dough on page 42.

1. Beat the eggs in a mixing bowl (or skip this step if you'd like to break the eggs directly onto the pies; see photo.)

2. Using your fingertips, raise the edges of the dough slightly to prevent the eggs from running.

3. If you are using a cast-iron crepe pan, griddle, or convex disc (*saj*), preheat over high heat. Heat the dough until small bubbles form; then lower the heat and melt the meat preserve in the middle of the dough for about 30 seconds, before spreading it evenly on the dough. Carefully crack or pour the eggs onto the dough and sprinkle with allspice and salt. Cook until the eggs are done and the edges are crisp, about 3 to 5 minutes, depending on the heat source. Lightly spray the cooking surface with water between pies, and wipe away any debris.

   If you are using a conventional oven, preheat the oven to 400°F (200°C / Gas mark 6). Spread the meat preserve onto the prepared dough, leaving about ½in (1cm) of exposed dough at the edges. Carefully crack or pour the eggs onto the dough and sprinkle with allspice and salt. Bake for 7 to 10 minutes on the bottom shelf until the eggs are cooked and the edges are slightly golden, watching carefully to make sure they don't burn.

4. Serve the pies hot.

 Yields 4 pies.

Meat Preserve Pie with Strained Yogurt

Awarma wa labneh

قورمة و لبنة

This pie is best cooked in the form of a stuffed half-moon shape in order to keep the moisture in.

Prepare the dough on page 42.

1 dough recipe (see p. 42)

1 cup (8oz / 240g) of meat preserve
(*awarma*, see p. 138)

1 cup (8oz / 240g) of strained yogurt
(*labneh*, see p. 85)

2 tablespoons of vegetable oil

1. Spread the *awarma* and *labneh* on one side of each prepared dough base, leaving about ½in (1cm) of exposed dough at the edges.

2. Fold the dough in half over the filling and pinch the edges together to make a half-moon shape.

3. Using a pastry brush, lightly coat the dough with vegetable oil.

4. If you are using a cast-iron crepe pan, griddle, or convex disc (*saj*), preheat over medium heat. Cook until the edges are golden, about 3 to 5 minutes, flipping over halfway through cooking. Lightly spray the cooking surface with water between pies, and wipe away any debris.

   If you are using a conventional oven, preheat the oven to 400°F (200°C / Gas mark 6). Bake for 7 to 10 minutes, flipping over halfway through cooking, until the edges are slightly golden, watching carefully to make sure they don't burn.

5. Serve the pies hot.

 Yields 4 pies.

☞ *Cook's Tip:* You can replace the *labneh* with the same quantity of whey cheese (*arisheh*).

► Nothing more delicious
than a *man'oushé*

▲ Serving customers with a smile.

▲ An early morning customer comes to the bakery in his sleeping attire.

قورما وكشك

Meat Preserve Pie with Kishk

Awarma wa kishk

If you like the taste of *kishk* and the taste of *awarma*, the combination is amazing. You won't be hungry for the rest of the day!

Prepare the dough on page 42.

1 dough recipe (see p. 42)

½ cup (2oz / 60g) of *kishk* (see p. 97)

2 medium tomatoes, finely chopped

1 medium onion, finely chopped or grated

1 teaspoon of tomato paste

½ cup (120ml) of olive oil

2 cups (14oz / 400g) of meat preserve (*awarma*, see p.138)

1. In a bowl, mix the *kishk* with the tomatoes, onion, tomato paste, and olive oil. You may need to add some water to loosen the mixture to a sauce-like consistency.

2. If you are using a cast-iron crepe pan, griddle, or convex disc (*saj*), preheat over high heat. Heat the dough until small bubbles form; then lower the heat, evenly spread the *kishk* mixture on the dough, then melt the meat preserve in the middle of the dough for about 30 seconds, before spreading it evenly. This method will prevent fat from running onto the cooking surface. Cook until the bottom is slightly golden and the edges are crisp, about 3 to 5 minutes, depending on the heat source. Lightly spray the cooking surface with water between pies, and wipe away any debris.

   If you are using a conventional oven, preheat the oven to 400°F (200°C / Gas mark 6). Spread the *kishk* mixture, then the meat preserve, carefully on the prepared dough, leaving about ½in (1cm) of exposed dough at the edges. Bake for 7 to 10 minutes on the bottom shelf until the dough is cooked and the bottom is slightly golden, watching carefully to make sure it does not burn.

3. Serve the pies hot.

🍲 *Yields 4 pies.*

 **Meat Preserve Pie with Hummus**

Awarma wa hommos bi-tahini

The hummus (*hommos bi-tahini*) melts into the hot meat preserve, making this pie an absolute treat.

FOR THE HUMMUS

1 cup (7oz / 200g) of dried chickpeas, soaked overnight in water and ½ teaspoon of baking soda (or 2 cups canned chickpeas), drained

½ cup (120ml) of sesame paste (*tahini*)

Juice of one lemon

1 or 2 cloves of garlic

1 teaspoon of salt

Makes about 2 cups

FOR THE PIE

1 dough recipe (see p. 42)

2 cups (14oz / 400g) of meat preserve (*awarma*, see p.138), approximately ½ cup for each pie

1 cup (8oz / 240g) of hummus (*hommos bi-tahini*), approximately ¼ cup for each pie

Pinch of cayenne pepper or paprika

Tomato slices and fresh mint leaves, to garnish

FOR THE HUMMUS (*HOMMOS BI-TAHINI*)

1. Bring a pan of water to a boil. Add the soaked, drained chickpeas and lower the heat. Simmer on low heat until tender, about 15–30 minutes. (I test them by squeezing one chickpea between my index finger and thumb). Drain the liquid, reserving about 1 cup.

2. Purée the chickpeas in a blender or food processor, slowly beating in the sesame paste and lemon juice alternately, tasting to make sure it is to your liking. If the mixture is too thick, add some of the reserved cooking liquid. Crush the garlic with the salt and mix it into the mixture. The hummus should be smooth and creamy.

FOR THE PIE

Prepare the dough on page 42.

1. If you are using a cast-iron crepe pan, griddle, or convex disc (*saj*), preheat over high heat. Heat the dough until small bubbles form; then lower the heat and melt the meat preserve in the middle of the dough for about 30 seconds, before spreading it evenly on the dough. This method will prevent fat from running onto the cooking surface. Cook until the bottom is slightly golden and the edges are crisp, about 3 to 5 minutes, depending on the heat source. Lightly spray the cooking surface with water between pies, and wipe away any debris.

   If you are using a conventional oven, preheat the oven to 400°F (200°C / Gas mark 6). Spread the meat preserve carefully on the prepared dough, leaving about ½in (1cm) of exposed dough at the edges. Bake for 7 to 10 minutes on the bottom shelf until the dough is slightly golden, watching carefully to make sure it does not burn.

2. When the pies are cooked, spread 2 tablespoons of hummus on each pie. Sprinkle the pie with a pinch of cayenne pepper or paprika.

3. Serve the pies hot, garnished with tomato slices and fresh mint.

Yields 4 pies.

> A stolen glimpse of a small bakery in the Shouf, owned by a young couple.

Meat
Lahmeh

اللحمة

Meat Pie

Red Pepper Paste

Aleppo Meat Pie

Armenian Meat Pie

Baalbek Bite-Sized Meat Pies

Meat Pie with Red Peppers

Bite-Sized Meat Pies with
Strained Yogurt

Tripoli Meat Pie

◀ Cooking meat pies on a convex disc (*saj*) makes for an open-air celebration.

▶ A *tannur* in a mud house built by the Issa family in Taanayel in the Beqa' Valley.

Meat Pie

Lahm bi-'ajeen

The *lahm bi-'ajeen* originates from Turkish and Armenian cuisine. The secret to a delicious *lahm bi-'ajeen* is to make the dough thin and crisp.

Prepare the dough on page 42, omitting the oil and sugar. Divide into 16 equal pieces and roll paper-thin (or you can roll the dough out and cut out the pieces using a cookie cutter or glass).

1 modified dough recipe (see p. 42)

2 medium onions

4 large or 6 medium tomatoes

1lb (500g) of finely-ground beef or lamb (75% lean, 25% fat for more flavor)

½ teaspoon of allspice

1½ teaspoons of salt

Pinch of black pepper

Lemon slices and red pepper paste (see p. 153), to garnish (optional)

1. Very finely chop the onions and tomatoes (or quarter them and pulse them in a food processor).

2. In a mixing bowl, combine the ground meat with the allspice, salt, and pepper. Mix the tomatoes and onions into the meat and knead to create a dough-like consistency.

3. Drain any excess liquid through a colander and divide the mixture into 16 pieces.

4. If you are using a cast-iron crepe pan, griddle, or convex disc (*saj*), preheat over low heat. Heat the dough until small bubbles form; then spread the meat over the whole surface of the dough. Cook on low heat (this ensures the meat cooks evenly) until the bottom is slightly golden and the edges are crisp, about 5 minutes, depending on the heat source. Lightly spray the cooking surface with water between batches, and wipe away any debris.

   If you are using a conventional oven, preheat the oven to 400°F (200°C / Gas mark 6). Spread the mixture over the whole surface of the prepared dough discs (the meat will shrink during cooking). Bake for 5 to 7 minutes on the bottom shelf until the edges are slightly golden, watching carefully so they don't burn.

5. Serve the pies hot with lemon slices, a pot of red pepper paste (for those who love spicy foods), and a glass of *ayran* (a drink made of diluted salted yogurt).

 Yields 16 pies.

▶ An assortment of red pepper pastes and spices in a small shop in Bourj Hammoud.

◀ Preparing my annual supply of red pepper paste in Ballouneh.

Red Pepper Paste

Ribb al-haar

This is something I enjoy making every year at the end of the summer. This year, to make my preserve more memorable, I went to 'Anjar, a village in the plain of the Beqa' Valley, mostly of Armenian inhabitants, to buy red peppers. I loaded up my car with sweet and hot red peppers and spent the whole next day making my red pepper paste. In the Lebanese restaurant I trained in, Chef Elie uses this paste to make a delicious dish called *batata haraa*: deep-fried potatoes marinated with garlic, olive oil, cilantro, and red pepper paste. The taste is out of this world! This red pepper paste is included in many recipes throughout the book. It is well worth making your own, as opposed to buying it commercially. The color, the texture, and the taste are different.

2 ¼lb (1kg) of hot red peppers

2 ¼lb (1kg) of sweet red peppers

2 tablespoons of coarse sea salt

½ cup (120ml) of olive oil (or more, depending on the jar you use)

1. Wash the peppers in cold water. Dry them carefully with a kitchen towel or leave them out in the sun for a couple of minutes.

2. Put on your gloves. Using a kitchen knife, slit the peppers in half and remove the seeds and membranes.

3. Pulse the peppers in a food processor or meat grinder until they are finely chopped.

4. Add the salt and stir to make sure that it seeps in. Transfer to a colander and leave to sweat for a couple of hours.

5. In a large pan, sauté the peppers in 1 teaspoon of olive oil until tender, about 15 minutes, and remove from the heat.

6. Transfer to a sterilized jar and allow to cool fully. Pour in enough olive oil to cover the top (this will seal in the flavor), cover, and refrigerate. The paste will last longer if you ensure it is always covered with olive oil.

Yields a 1qt / 1kg jar

Cook's Tip: I make my red pepper paste medium-hot. If you like it hotter, add more hot peppers and reduce the amount of sweet peppers. It is worth mentioning that making this paste can be very enjoyable, but one must be careful when working with hot peppers. Wear gloves at all times and be careful not to touch your face or skin. Thoroughly wash any equipment that has been exposed to the hot peppers. Keep children away.

Aleppo Meat Pie

Lahm bi-'ajeen Halabi

لحم بعجين حلبي

Aleppo is a large city in the north of Syria. Its name has resonated in my ears since my childhood, when my parents told me stories of their parents' childhood in this magnificent city. But it never meant anything to me until I visited. It is a grand city, full of history, splendor, and life. What struck me the most was the culinary expertise and the delicious meat dishes. I lean towards a vegetarian way of life, but in Aleppo, I ate more meat than I had eaten in a lifetime.

Prepare the dough on page 42, omitting the oil and sugar. Divide dough into 16 equal pieces and roll paper-thin (or you can roll the dough out and cut out the pieces using a cookie cutter or glass).

1 modified dough recipe (see p. 42)

2 medium onions

1 small tomato to soften the mixture (optional)

1lb (500g) of finely-ground beef or lamb (75% lean, 25% fat for more flavor)

½ teaspoon of allspice

1½ teaspoons of salt

Pinch of black pepper

1 tablespoon of sesame paste (*tahini*)

3 tablespoons (45ml) of sour pomegranate syrup

½ cup (2oz / 50g) of pine nuts

1. Very finely chop the onions and tomato, if using (or quarter them and pulse them in a food processor).

2. In a mixing bowl, combine the ground meat, onions, and tomato with the allspice, salt, and pepper. Pour in the sesame paste and the pomegranate syrup and add the pine nuts. Knead to create a dough-like consistency. (The mixture should be a dark color.)

3. Divide the mixture into 16 parts.

4. If you are using a cast-iron crepe pan, griddle, or convex disc (*saj*), preheat over low heat. Heat the dough until small bubbles form; then spread the meat over the whole surface of the dough. Cook on low heat (this ensures the meat cooks evenly) until the bottom is slightly golden and the edges are crisp, about 5 minutes, depending on the heat source. Lightly spray the cooking surface with water between pies, and wipe away any debris.

   If you are using a conventional oven, preheat the oven to 400°F (200°C / Gas mark 6). Spread the mixture over the whole surface of the prepared dough (the meat will shrink during cooking). Bake for 5 to 7 minutes on the bottom shelf until the edges are slightly golden, watching carefully so they don't burn.

5. Serve the pies hot.

 Yields 16 pies.

▶ A butcher in Shatila, in the suburbs of Beirut.

◄ Café Garo in Bourj Hammoud, where you can find a wide variety of specialized foods and spices.

► The best way to spread the meat mixture is with your fingertips.

Armenian Meat Pie

Lahm bi-'ajeen Armaneh

According to my son, this is the best meat pie he's ever had in his life. I always believe the truth comes out of the mouths of children.

Prepare the dough on page 42, omitting the oil and sugar. Divide dough into 16 equal pieces and roll paper-thin (or you can roll the dough out and cut out the pieces using a cookie cutter or glass). Use a generous amount of flour while you work with the dough.

1 modified dough recipe (see p. 42)

2 medium onions

4 to 5 garlic cloves

4 large or 6 medium tomatoes

½ green pepper

½ bunch of flat-leaf parsley

1lb (500g) of finely-ground beef or lamb (75% lean, 25% fat for more flavor)

1 teaspoon to 1 tablespoon of red pepper paste, or to taste

½ teaspoon of allspice

1½ teaspoons of salt

Pinch of black pepper

½ cup (2oz / 50g) of pine nuts (optional)

Lemon juice or red pepper powder, to garnish

1. Finely chop the onions, garlic, tomatoes, bell pepper, and parsley (or quarter the vegetables and pulse them in a food processor; the parsley must be chopped by hand).

2. In a mixing bowl, combine the ground meat with the red pepper paste, allspice, salt, pepper, and pine nuts, if using. Mix the vegetables and parsley into the meat and knead to create a dough-like consistency.

3. Strain excess liquid through a colander and divide the mixture into 16 parts.

4. If you are using a cast-iron crepe pan, griddle, or convex disc (*saj*), preheat over low heat. Heat the dough until small bubbles form; then spread the meat over the whole surface of the dough. Cook on low heat (this ensures the meat cooks evenly) until the bottom is slightly golden and the edges are crisp, about 5 minutes, depending on the heat source. Lightly spray the cooking surface with water between pies, and wipe away any debris.

   If you are using a conventional oven, preheat the oven to 400°F (200°C / Gas mark 6). Spread the mixture over the whole surface of the prepared dough (the meat will shrink during cooking). Bake for 5 to 7 minutes on the bottom shelf until the edges are slightly golden, watching carefully so they don't burn.

5. Serve the pies hot with a squeeze of lemon juice or a pinch of red pepper powder.

 Yields 16 pies.

Baalbek Bite-Sized Meat Pies

Sfiha b'albakieh

صفيحة بعلبكية

Baalbek is located in the rich and fertile Beqa' Valley. It is Lebanon's greatest Roman treasure. People come from all over the world to visit the site and eat these bite-sized meat pies; they are truly a delicacy.

Prepare the dough on page 42, adding 1 tablespoon of ghee or butter. Divide dough into 16–20 equal pieces and roll each piece to a 3–4in (7–10cm) circle with a thickness of about ⅛in (10mm).

1 modified dough recipe (see p. 42)

2 medium onions

4 large or 6 medium tomatoes

1lb (500g) of finely-ground beef or lamb
(75% lean, 25% fat for more flavor)

½ teaspoon of allspice

1½ teaspoons of salt

Pinch of black pepper

1. Very finely chop the onions and tomatoes (or quarter them and pulse them in a food processor).

2. In a mixing bowl, combine the ground meat, allspice, salt, and pepper. Mix the tomatoes and onions into the meat and knead to create a dough-like consistency. Drain any excess liquid through a colander.

3. Place a spoonful of meat mixture in the center of each circle of dough. Fold the edges of the circle over the meat, leaving the center exposed. Pinch the edges together to form a square (see picture). Let the pies stand for 15 minutes before cooking.

4. Place the pies on a lightly-oiled baking tray and preheat the oven to 400°F (200°C / Gas mark 6).

5. Bake for 15 to 20 minutes on the bottom shelf until the edges are slightly golden, watching carefully so they don't burn.

6. The pies can be eaten at room temperature, but are much tastier hot out of the oven.

Yields 16–20 bite-sized pies.

Variation: Another way to make these bite-sized pies is to replace the tomatoes with ½ cup (2oz / 50g) of pine nuts, ½ cup (4oz / 120g) of yogurt, 3 tablespoons (45ml) of sour pomegranate syrup, and 1 tablespoon of sesame paste (*tahini*).

► Large mounds of dough are kneaded carefully in this machine called an *'ejjeneh*.

◀ A priest is called upon to bless a snack in Hrajel, in the high mountains of Kesserouan.

▶ Sweet red peppers dried in the sun.

Meat Pie with Red Peppers

خبز لحم حرة

Lahm bi-'ajeen ma' flayfleh harra

This recipe is for red pepper lovers! I use both sweet and hot peppers. You can choose to use sweet or hot individually.

Prepare the dough on page 42, omitting the oil and sugar. Divide dough into 16 equal pieces and roll paper-thin (or you can roll the dough out and cut out the pieces using a cookie cutter or glass). Use a generous amount of flour while you work with the dough.

1 modified dough recipe (see p. 42)

2 medium onions

4 to 5 garlic cloves

4 large or 6 medium tomatoes

1 medium sweet red pepper

2 small hot red chili peppers

½ large bunch of flat-leaf parsley, finely chopped

1lb (500g) of finely-ground beef or lamb (75% lean, 25% fat for more flavor)

1 teaspoon of red pepper paste (see p. 153)

1 teaspoon of tomato paste

½ teaspoon of allspice

1½ teaspoons of salt

Pinch of black pepper

1. Finely chop the onions, garlic, tomatoes, and peppers (or quarter the vegetables and pulse them in a food processor; the parsley must be chopped by hand).

2. In a mixing bowl, combine the ground meat with the red pepper paste, tomato paste, allspice, salt, and pepper. Mix in the parsley and vegetables and knead to create a dough-like consistency.

3. Strain excess liquid through a colander and divide the mixture into 16 parts.

4. If you are using a cast-iron crepe pan, griddle, or convex disc (*saj*), preheat over low heat. Heat the dough until small bubbles form; then spread the meat over the whole surface of the dough. Cook on low heat (this ensures the meat cooks evenly) until the bottom is slightly golden and the edges are crisp, about 5 minutes, depending on the heat source. Lightly spray the cooking surface with water between pies, and wipe away any debris.

   If you are using a conventional oven, preheat the oven to 400°F (200°C / Gas mark 6). Spread the mixture over the whole surface of the prepared dough (the meat will shrink during cooking). Bake for 5 to 7 minutes on the bottom shelf until the edges are slightly golden, watching carefully so they don't burn.

5. Serve the pies hot.

 Yields 16 pies.

◀ Cheesecloth full of yogurt (*laban*) drained over a kitchen sink.

▶ Proud owner of Hamadeh bakery in Hamra.

Bite-Sized Meat Pies with Strained Yogurt

Sfiha bi-labneh

صفيحة بلبنة

This recipe brings back teenage memories of swinging on the balcony at my friend's Mireille's house, looking out with melancholy at the Bay of Beirut. Mireille's mother, Mona, loves to bake and feed her family and friends. When she made these bite-sized meat pies, they would disappear instantly.

Prepare the dough on page 42, adding 1 tablespoon of ghee or butter. Divide dough into 16–20 equal pieces before rolling out each piece to a 3–4in (7–10cm) circle with a thickness of about ⅛in (10mm).

1 modified dough recipe (see p. 42)

¼ cup (60ml) of vegetable oil

½ cup (2oz / 50g) of pine nuts

2 medium onions, finely chopped

1lb (500g) of finely-ground beef or lamb (75% lean, 25% fat for more flavor)

½ teaspoon of allspice

Pinch of cinnamon

Pinch of black pepper

1½ teaspoons of salt

½ cup (4oz / 115g) of strained yogurt (*labneh*, see p. 85)

Juice of 1 lemon

1. In a frying pan, heat the oil over medium heat. Sauté the pine nuts until golden brown. Drain on paper towels, reserving the oil.

2. Fry the onions in the reserved oil until translucent, stirring regularly. Add the meat, spices, and seasoning, and cook until browned, about 5 minutes, being careful not to overcook.

3. Set aside to cool. Add the *labneh* and the lemon juice and mix well.

4. Place a spoonful of meat mixture in the center of each circle of dough. Fold the edges of the circle over the meat, leaving the center exposed. Pinch the edges together to form a square (see picture on p.158). Let the pies stand for 15 minutes before cooking.

5. Place the pies on a lightly-oiled baking tray and preheat the oven to 400°F (200°C / Gas mark 6).

6. Bake for 15 to 20 minutes on the bottom shelf until the edges are slightly golden, watching carefully so they don't burn.

7. The pies can be eaten at room temperature, but are much tastier hot out of the oven.

Yields 16–20 bite-sized pieces.

Tripoli Meat Pies

Sfiha Traboulsieh

عجينة طرابلسية

The city of Tripoli, about 50 miles (85km) north of Beirut, is known for its delicious Arabic sweets. One famous pastry shop called Abdel Rahman al Hallab very generously invited me inside the kitchen to learn the recipe and technique for this delicious savory pie.

2 medium onions

1lb (500g) of finely-ground beef or lamb (75% lean, 25% fat for more flavor)

1 tablespoon of vinegar

1 tablespoon of sesame paste (*tahini*)

3 tablespoons (45ml) of sour pomegranate syrup

½ cup (4oz / 50g) of pine nuts

½ teaspoon of allspice

1½ teaspoons of salt

Pinch of black pepper

1lb (450g) package of puff pastry, thawed if frozen (follow manufacturer's instructions)

Lemon wedges, to garnish

1. Finely chop the onions (or quarter them and pulse in a food processor). Transfer to a large bowl and mix in the ground meat, vinegar, sesame paste, sour pomegranate syrup, pine nuts, allspice, salt, and pepper. Knead to create a dough-like consistency.

2. Carefully unroll the pastry dough. Cut into 4in (10cm) squares (or whatever size you desire).

3. Place a spoonful of meat mixture in the center of each square and spread, leaving a small crust of exposed dough at the edges.

4. Place the pies on a lightly-oiled baking tray and preheat the oven to 400°F (200°C / Gas mark 6). Bake for 15 to 20 minutes on the bottom shelf (or follow the manufacturer's cooking instructions) until the meat is cooked and the pastry is flaky and golden.

5. Serve the pies hot with lemon wedges.

Yields 4 pies.

◀ Ancient souk of Tripoli.

الكفتة

Ground Meat, Onion, & Parsley

Kafta

Ground Meat, Onion, and
Parsley Pie

Raw Meat, Onion, and Parsley Pie

Ground Meat, Onion, and Parsley
Pie with Hummus

Ground Meat, Onion, and Parsley
Pie with Red Pepper Paste

Ground Meat, Onion, & Parsley Pie

فتة

Kafta

Kafta is a popular meal in Lebanon. You can even bring a fresh bunch of parsley and peeled onions to the butcher to have it prepared on the spot. The mixture can be baked in the oven with a layer of potatoes and tomatoes, grilled on skewers, or simply cooked in a frying pan. Here, I have adapted the recipe to make a pie that is fragrant and delicious.

Prepare the dough on page 42. Divide into 8 equal pieces and roll thinly.

1 modified dough recipe (see p. 42)

2 medium onions

½ large bunch of flat-leaf parsley

1lb (500g) of finely-ground beef or lamb (75% lean, 25% fat for more flavor)

½ teaspoon of allspice

½ teaspoon of seven spice

Pinch of cinnamon

Pinch of nutmeg

1½ teaspoons of salt

Pinch of black pepper

1 lemon, sliced into wedges and ½ green pepper, sliced, to garnish (optional)

1. Finely chop the onions and parsley leaves.

2. In a bowl, combine the ground meat with the spice, salt, and pepper. Mix in the chopped onions and parsley. Knead to create a dough-like consistency.

3. Divide the mixture into 8 parts and spread over the whole surface of the dough circles.

4. If you are using a cast-iron crepe pan, griddle, or convex disc (*saj*), preheat over low heat. Cook on low heat (this ensures the meat cooks evenly) until the bottom is slightly golden and the edges are crisp, about 5 minutes, depending on the heat source. Lightly spray the cooking surface with water between pies, and wipe away any debris.

   If you are using a conventional oven, preheat the oven to 400°F (200°C / Gas mark 6). Bake for 5 to 7 minutes on the bottom shelf until the edges are slightly golden, watching carefully so they don't burn.

5. Serve the pies hot with a squeeze of fresh lemon juice and slices of green pepper or any vegetable that you particularly like.

 Yields 8 pies.

☞ *Cook's Tip:* You can add ¼ large bunch of fresh mint, finely chopped, to the vegetables. You can also top each pie with 1 tablespoon of pine nuts before cooking. Alternatively, layer on slices of *'akkawi* cheese in an attractive diagonal pattern.

Raw Meat, Onion, & Parsley Pie

Kafta nayeh

For this pie, make sure that the meat you use is very fresh. Tell your butcher that this meat will be eaten raw. This is why I always insist on the importance of having a friendly relationship with one's butcher. I first tasted *kafta nayeh* in the mountains of Ehmez in a family-owned Lebanese restaurant. Nearby, my father-in-law still farms the land of his forefathers.

Prepare the dough on page 42. Divide into 8 equal pieces and roll thinly.

1 modified dough recipe (see p. 42)

2 medium onions (plus more for garnish)

½ large bunch of flat-leaf parsley

1lb (500g) of finely-ground beef or lamb (75% lean, 25% fat for more flavor)

½ teaspoon of allspice

½ teaspoon of seven spice

Pinch of cinnamon

Pinch of nutmeg

Pinch of black pepper

1½ teaspoons of salt

Onion wedges, sliced tomatoes, fresh mint, and sumac, to garnish (optional)

1. Very finely chop the onions and parsley (or you can quarter the onions and pulse them in a food processor).

2. In a mixing bowl, combine the ground meat, spices, and seasoning. Mix in the onions and parsley and knead to create a dough-like consistency.

3. Tap the dough with your fingertips or prick with a fork to prevent air pockets from forming.

4. If you are using a cast-iron crepe pan, griddle, or convex disc (*saj*), preheat over high heat. Cook each circle of dough until the bottom is slightly golden and the edges are crisp, about 3 to 5 minutes, depending on the heat source. Lightly spray the cooking surface with water between pies, and wipe away any debris.

   If you are using a conventional oven, preheat the oven to 425°F (220°C / Gas mark 7). Bake the dough for 5 to 7 minutes on the bottom shelf, watching carefully to make sure it does not burn.

5. Divide the meat mixture into 8 equal parts, and spread over the cooked dough.

6. Serve the pies with onion wedges, sliced tomatoes, fresh mint leaves, and a sprinkle of sumac, if desired.

 Yields 8 pies.

▶ In the crowded streets of Bourj Hammoud, this man quietly enjoys his meal.

◀ This man has been running a snack in Tripoli for over 30 years.

Ground Meat, Onion, & Parsley Pie with Hummus

Kafta wa hommos bi-tahini

Hummus *(hommos bi-tahini)* is one of the most important dishes that make up the Lebanese *mezze*. It is a delightful topping that complements the *kafta* pie. Try it—you'll love it!

Prepare the dough on page 42. Divide into 8 equal pieces and roll thinly.

1 modified dough recipe (see p. 42)

2 medium onions (plus more for garnish, if desired)

½ large bunch of flat-leaf parsley

1lb (500g) of finely-ground beef or lamb (75% lean, 25% fat for more flavor)

½ teaspoon of allspice

½ teaspoon of seven spice

Pinch of cinnamon

Pinch of nutmeg

Pinch of black pepper

1½ teaspoons of salt

1 cup (8oz / 240g) of hummus (*hommos bi-tahini*, see p.146)

A handful of cooked chickpeas and a pinch of red pepper powder, to garnish (optional)

1. Finely chop the onions and parsley.

2. In a bowl, combine the ground meat with the spices, salt, and pepper. Mix in the chopped onions and parsley and knead to create a dough-like consistency.

3. Divide the mixture into 8 parts and spread over the whole surface of the dough circles.

4. If you are using a cast-iron crepe pan, griddle, or convex disc (*saj*), preheat over low heat. Cook on low heat (this ensures the meat cooks evenly) until the bottom is slightly golden and the edges are crisp, about 5 minutes, depending on the heat source. Lightly spray the cooking surface with water between pies, and wipe away any debris.

   If you are using a conventional oven, preheat the oven to 400°F (200°C / Gas mark 6). Bake for 5 to 7 minutes on the bottom shelf until the edges are slightly golden, watching carefully so they don't burn.

5. Cool slightly. Spread 2 tablespoons of hummus on each pie before serving. Top with the garnish, if using.

 Yields 8 pies.

☞ *Cook's Tip:* You can finely chop ¼ to ½ bunch of fresh mint and add it to the meat mixture. You can also top each pie with 1 tablespoon of pine nuts before cooking.

 ## Ground Meat, Onion, & Parsley Pie with Red Pepper Paste

Kafta wa ribb al-haar

The red pepper paste adds spice, flavor, and color to this pie.

Prepare the dough on page 42. Divide into 8 equal pieces and roll thinly.

1 modified dough recipe (see p. 42)

2 medium onions

½ bunch of flat-leaf parsley

1lb (500g) of finely-ground beef or lamb (75% lean, 25% fat for more flavor)

½ teaspoon of allspice

½ teaspoon of seven spice

Pinch of black pepper

Pinch of cinnamon

Pinch of nutmeg

1½ teaspoons of salt

1 teaspoon to 1 tablespoon of red pepper paste (see p. 153)

1. Finely chop the onions and parsley.

2. In a bowl, combine the ground meat with the spices. Mix in the chopped onions and parsley and knead to create a dough-like consistency. Divide the mixture into 8 parts.

3. Spread the red pepper paste onto the prepared dough circles, then spread the meat mixture on top. (Alternatively, you can spoon it onto the middle of each cooked pie).

4. If you are using a cast-iron crepe pan, griddle, or convex disc (*saj*), preheat over low heat. Cook on low heat (this ensures the meat cooks evenly) until the bottom is slightly golden and the edges are crisp, about 5 minutes, depending on the heat source. Lightly spray the cooking surface with water between pies, and wipe away any debris.

   If you are using a conventional oven, preheat the oven to 400°F (200°C / Gas mark 6). Bake for 5 to 7 minutes on the bottom shelf until the edges are slightly golden, watching carefully so they don't burn.

5. Serve the pies hot.

 Yields 8 pies.

▶ Parking attendant enjoying his breakfast. Sign reads "Prompt payment, no postponement"

Armenian
Sausage

السجق

Sujuk

Armenian Sausage Pie

Armenian Sausage Pie with Cheese

Armenian Sausage Pie with Eggs

Armenian Sausage Pie

Sujuk

Sujuk sausages, introduced by the Armenian community, have become a part of Lebanese cuisine. I visited local merchants in Bourj Hammoud, where you can see the colorful sausages hanging everywhere. The *sujuk* sausage is a strong-tasting, air-dried lamb or beef sausage seasoned with red chili pepper flakes, cumin, paprika, allspice, cinnamon, garlic, and salt. If you can't find *sujuk*, you can use chorizo or your favorite cured sausage.

1 dough recipe (see p. 42)

½lb (250g) *sujuk* sausages, sliced into thin discs (number needed depends on the size)

Sliced green peppers and / or tomatoes for garnish

Prepare the dough on page 42.

1. Arrange the sausage slices on the prepared dough.

2. If you are using a cast-iron crepe pan, griddle, or convex disc (*saj*), preheat over medium heat. Place a pie onto the hot surface and cook until the bottom is slightly golden and the edges are crisp, 3 to 5 minutes, depending on the heat source. Lightly spray the cooking surface with water between pies, and wipe away any debris.

   If you are using a conventional oven, preheat the oven to 400°F (200°C / Gas mark 6). Bake for 7 to 10 minutes on the bottom shelf until the edges are slightly golden, watching carefully so they don't burn.

3. Serve the pies hot, topped with sliced green peppers and / or tomatoes.

 Yields 4 pies.

◄ Two friendly locals on the streets of Bourj Hammoud.

Armenian Sausage Pie with Cheese

سجق وجبنة

Sujuk wa jibneh

For this pie, I prefer to use mild cheeses like mozzarella or mild white cheddar. They melt easily and do not overpower the taste of the *sujuk*.

Prepare the dough on page 42.

1 dough recipe (see p. 42)

½lb (250g) *sujuk* sausages, sliced into thin discs (number needed depends on the size)

3½ cups (8oz / 225g) of grated cheese (mozzarella, mild white cheddar, or similar mild white cheese)

Mint leaves and tomato slices, to garnish (optional)

1. Arrange the sausage slices on the prepared dough and top with grated cheese.

2. If you are using a cast-iron crepe pan, griddle, or convex disc (*saj*), preheat over medium heat. Place a pie onto the hot surface and cook until the bottom is slightly golden and the edges are crisp, 3 to 5 minutes depending on the heat source. Lightly spray the cooking surface with water between pies, and wipe away any debris.

   If you are using a conventional oven, preheat the oven to 400°F (200°C / Gas mark 6). Bake for 7 to 10 minutes on the bottom shelf until the edges are slightly golden, watching carefully so they don't burn.

3. Serve the pies hot, topped with mint leaves and tomato slices, if using.

 Yields 4 pies.

Armenian Sausage Pie with Eggs

Sujuk wa bayd

سجق وبيض

The flavor of the Armenian sausage goes very well with eggs. This pie makes a hearty breakfast!

Prepare the dough on page 42.

1 dough recipe (see p. 42)

8 large eggs (2 eggs for each pie), at room temperature

½lb (250g) *sujuk* sausages, sliced into thin discs (number needed depends on the size)

1. Beat the eggs in a mixing bowl (or skip this step if you'd like to break the eggs directly onto the pies).

2. Using your fingertips, raise the edges of the dough slightly to prevent the eggs from running onto the cooking surface.

3. Arrange the sausage slices on the prepared dough.

4. If you are using a cast-iron crepe pan, griddle, or convex disc (*saj*), preheat over medium heat. Place a topped pie onto the hot surface. Carefully crack or pour the eggs onto the sausages. Cook until the eggs are cooked and the edges are crisp, about 3 to 5 minutes, depending on the heat source. Lightly spray the cooking surface with water between pies, and wipe away any debris.

   If you are using a conventional oven, preheat the oven to 400°F (200°C / Gas mark 6). Carefully crack or pour the eggs onto the sausages. Bake for 7 to 10 minutes on the bottom shelf until the eggs are cooked and the edges are slightly golden, watching carefully so they don't burn.

5. Serve the pies hot.

 Yields 4 pies.

الحلو **Sweet**

Helou

Chocolate Pie

Halawa Pie

Molasses and Sesame Paste Pie

Whey Cheese Pie with Honey

Sesame Seed Bread

Sesame Paste Bread

Ramadan Bread

Chocolate Pie

Chocolata

شوكولاته

A favorite with kids, and I know a few hundred adults who love this pie too—including my husband!

Prepare the dough on page 42.

1 dough recipe (see p. 42)

1 cup (8oz / 250g) of chocolate sauce or spread (about ¼ cup per pie)

Chopped nuts or sliced bananas, to garnish (optional)

1. Tap the dough with your fingertips or prick with a fork to prevent air pockets from forming.

2. If you are using a cast-iron crepe pan, griddle, or convex disc (*saj*), preheat over high heat. Cook each circle of dough until the bottom is slightly golden and the edges are crisp, about 3 to 5 minutes, depending on the heat source. Lightly spray the cooking surface with water between pies, and wipe away any debris.

   If you are using a conventional oven, preheat the oven to 425°F (220°C / Gas mark 7). Bake the dough for 5 to 7 minutes on the bottom shelf, watching carefully to make sure it does not burn.

3. Allow the bread discs to cool slightly before evenly spreading the chocolate over each one.

4. If desired, you can top the pie with sliced bananas or chopped nuts.

5. Serve warm or at room temperature.

 Yields 4 pies.

▶ Mia and Sarah, my daughters, preparing dough.

A beautiful fifteen-year-old girl from the Beqa' Valley operates a bakery in Broumana in the Metn.

Halawa Pie

Halaweh

Halva *(halawa)* is a coarse paste made using the roots of the halva plant (*Saponaria* or soapwort). Through a number of cooking procedures, we obtain the root extract (*natef*), which is combined with sesame paste (*tahini*). You can also find *halawa* with pistachios, almonds, or chocolate. Its flavor is sweet with a hint of bitterness.

Prepare the dough on page 42.

1 dough recipe (see p. 42)

1 cup (5oz / 150g) of halva (*halawa*), about ¼ cup per pie

1 tablespoon of vegetable oil

1. In a bowl, crumble the *halawa* with your fingers.

2. Sprinkle the *halawa* onto half of each disc of dough, leaving about ½in (1cm) of exposed dough at the edges. Fold the disc in half over the filling to make a half-moon shape. Carefully pinch the edges together using your index finger and thumb. This method will prevent the *halawa* from drying out during cooking.

3. Using a pastry brush, lightly coat the dough with vegetable oil.

4. If you are using a cast-iron crepe pan, griddle, or convex disc (*saj*), preheat over medium heat. Cook until the edges are golden, about 3 to 5 minutes, flipping over halfway through cooking. Lightly spray the cooking surface with water between pies, and wipe away any debris.

   If you are using a conventional oven, preheat the oven to 400°F (200°C / Gas mark 6). Bake for 7 to 10 minutes, flipping over halfway through cooking, until the edges are slightly golden, watching carefully to make sure they don't burn.

5. Serve at room temperature.

 Yields 4 pies.

▶ Partners in crime, Albert Senior and Junior!

دبس بطحينة **Molasses and Sesame Paste Pie**

Debs bi-tahini

My father-in-law makes a rich molasses paste (*debs*) from aging raisins from his garden. I always rejoice when he offers me one of his homemade jars. The combination of *debs* and *tahini* makes this pie a rich and delicious dessert. It's my favorite!

Prepare the dough on page 42.

1 dough recipe (see p. 42)

1 cup (250ml) of raisin or carob molasses (*debs*), about ¼ cup per pie

½ cup (120ml) of sesame paste (*tahini*), about ¼ cup per pie

1. Tap the dough with your fingertips or prick with a fork to prevent air pockets from forming.

2. If you are using a cast-iron crepe pan, griddle, or convex disc (*saj*), preheat over high heat. Cook each circle of dough until the bottom is slightly golden and the edges are crisp, about 3 to 5 minutes, depending on the heat source. Lightly spray the cooking surface with water between pies, and wipe away any debris.

   If you are using a conventional oven, preheat the oven to 425°F (220°C / Gas mark 7). Bake the dough for 5 to 7 minutes on the bottom shelf, watching carefully to make sure it does not burn.

3. Spread the molasses over the cooked dough. Drizzle with sesame paste.

4. Serve at room temperature.

 Yields 4 pies.

Whey Cheese Pie with Honey

قريشة وعسل

Arisheh wa 'asal

Arisheh is a whey cheese resembling ricotta. This cheese mixed with honey is typically served at Lebanese restaurants after an extensive meal. They offer a plate of *arisheh* with honey accompanied by an appetizing platter of seasonal fresh fruits for dessert. Another example of Lebanese hospitality!

Prepare the dough on page 42.

1 dough recipe (see p. 42)

2 cups (1lb / 500g) of *arisheh* (or substitute ricotta)

1 cup (250ml) of honey

1. Tap the dough with your fingertips or prick with a fork to prevent air pockets from forming.

2. If you are using a cast-iron crepe pan, griddle, or convex disc (*saj*), preheat over high heat. Cook each circle of dough until the bottom is slightly golden and the edges are crisp, about 3 to 5 minutes, depending on the heat source. Lightly spray the cooking surface with water between pies, and wipe away any debris.

   If you are using a conventional oven, preheat the oven to 425°F (220°C / Gas mark 7). Bake the dough for 5 to 7 minutes on the bottom shelf, watching carefully to make sure it does not burn.

3. Spread the *arisheh* over the cooked dough. Drizzle with honey.

4. Serve at room temperature.

 Yields 4 pies.

> ▶ Chafika Harb (Oum Najib) from Deir el Tahnish, serving Arabic coffee the Lebanese way.

BAKERY
JEDDO
SOUSOU
FREE DELIVERY
تأمين جميع
أنواع المعجنات
للمناسبات
07/ 425566

Sesame Seed Bread

Khobz bi- sumsum

Sweet and delicious, this bread makes a great snack!

Prepare the dough on page 42.

1 dough recipe (see p. 42)

¼ cup (60ml) of oil, butter, or ghee (1 tablespoon for each pie)

¼ cup (50g) of sugar (1 tablespoon for each pie)

¼ cup (1oz / 40g) of raw sesame seeds (1 tablespoon for each pie)

1. Spread oil or butter on the prepared dough and sprinkle on the sugar.

2. Roll the dough into a thin rope around the sugar.

3. Curl the rope into a swirl.

4. Dip the top of the swirl into the sesame seeds and press gently so they stick.

5. It is preferable to cook this pie in a conventional cooking oven (the sesame seeds will burn more easily on a griddle or convex disc). Preheat the oven to 425°F (220°C / Gas mark 7). Bake the dough for 7 to 10 minutes on the bottom shelf, watching carefully to make sure the seeds don't burn.

6. Serve at room temperature.

 Yields 4 loaves.

Sesame Paste Bread

Khobz bi-tahini

During the Christian period of Lent, various bakeries cease to make meat pies. Armenian bakeries make this rich bread as a substitute.

Prepare the dough on page 42, omitting the oil and sugar.

1 modified dough recipe (see p. 42)

1 cup (8oz / 250g) of sesame paste (*tahini*)

½ cup (4oz / 110g) of sugar

2 teaspoons of cinnamon (about ½ teaspoon for each pie)

1. Spread the sesame paste onto each prepared dough base. Sprinkle with sugar, then cinnamon.

2. Roll the dough into a thin rope around the fillings.

3. Curl the rope into a swirl.

4. If you are using a cast-iron crepe pan, griddle, or convex disc (*saj*), preheat over high heat. Cook each swirl until the edges are slightly golden, about 3 to 5 minutes, flipping over halfway through cooking. Lightly spray the cooking surface with water between pies, and wipe away any debris.

   If you are using a conventional oven, preheat the oven to 425°F (220°C / Gas mark 7). Bake the swirls for 7 to 10 minutes on the bottom shelf, until the edges are slightly golden, watching carefully to make sure they don't burn.

5. Serve at room temperature.

Yields 4 loaves.

▲ This couple from Shiah named their bakery Tam-Tam after their daughter's nickname.

▲ At Mrs. Ichkhanian's bakery, preparing a large order of *tahini* bread.

▶ An old fire-glazed oven in the valley of Wadi Qannoubine in the north of Lebanon.

Ramadan Bread

Mishtah

مشطاح

Ramadan is a period of fasting in the Islamic faith. During the month of Ramadan, this bread is commonly served in bakeries. The first time I tried it, on my way to the south of Lebanon, I was served this delicious bread wrapped in a newspaper. Here they called the bread *mishtah*.

Follow the method on page 42, adding the ground anise seeds, powdered milk, and ground mahlab, at step 2. Divide into 2 equal pieces. Roll each piece into a disc of about 12in (30cm) with a thickness of about ½in (1cm).

2½ cups (13oz / 360g) of white bread (strong) flour

1 cup (5oz / 150g) of cake flour

1 teaspoon of active dry yeast

1¼ cups (300ml) of lukewarm water (body temperature is best)

2 teaspoons of salt

1 tablespoon of sugar

¼ teaspoon of ground anise seeds

1 tablespoon of powdered whole (full-fat) milk

½ teaspoon of ground *mahlab*

1 tablespoon of vegetable oil

½ cup (2oz / 60g) of butter

2 tablespoons of nigella seeds

4 tablespoons of raw sesame seeds

1. To decorate the bread with a crosshatch design, pinch the dough discs in even parallel strips using your index finger and thumb, first vertically, then horizontally.

2. Using a pastry brush, brush the dough with melted butter.

3. Sprinkle the dough with nigella seeds and white sesame seeds in any pattern you desire.

4. It is preferable to cook this pie in a conventional cooking oven (the sesame seeds will burn more easily on a griddle or convex disc). Preheat the oven to 425°F (220°C / Gas mark 7). Bake the dough on the bottom shelf until the edges are golden, about 7 to 10 minutes.

5. Serve hot or at room temperature.

Yields 2 loaves.

◄ Preparation of *mishtah* during the holy month of Ramadan in the souk of Baalbek.

Index فهرس

Aleppo Meat Pie 154
Arabic Bread (khobz 'Arabi) 44–45
Armenian Meat Pie 157
Armenian Sausage (sujuk) 32, 177
   Armenian Sausage Pie 179
   Armenian Sausage Pie with Cheese 180
   Armenian Sausage Pie with Eggs 181
awarma see Meat Preserve

Baalbek Bite-Sized Meat Pies 158
beef see meat
Bite-Sized Meat Pies with Strained Yogurt 162
bread (khobz)
   Arabic Bread (khobz 'Arabi) 44–45
   Paper-Thin Bread (khobz marquq) 47–48
   Sesame Seed Bread 193
   Sesame Paste Bread 194
   Ramadan Bread 197
bulgar (burghul) 31 see also Dried Yogurt
   and Bulgar (kishk)
   Wild Thyme Pie with Whole-Wheat Flour and
      Bulgar Dough 63
Bulgari Cheese Pie 81
burghul see bulgar

Cheese (jibneh) 32, 69 see also strained yogurt (labneh)
   'akkawi see white cheese
   arisheh see whey cheese
   Bulgari 32
      Bulgari Cheese Pie 81
   feta 32
      Feta Cheese Pie 83
   halloumi 32
      Supreme Cheese Pie 72
   kashkaval 32
      Kashkaval Cheese Pie 83
   Spiced Cheese Balls (shankleesh) 32, 77
      Spiced Cheese Pie 78
      Spiced Cheese Pie with White Cheese 79
   white cheese ('akkawi) 32
      Cheese Pie 71
      Supreme Cheese Pie 72
      Hot Cheese Pie 75
      Cheese Pie with Vegetables 76
      Spiced Cheese Pie with White Cheese 79
   whey cheese (arisheh) 32
      Whey Cheese Pie 91
      Whey Cheese Pie with Honey 190
Chicken (djeij) 131
   Chicken Pie 132
   Chicken Pie with Cilantro and Garlic 135
chickpeas (hboub hommos) see also hummus
   Chickpea Pie 122
   Ground Meat, Onion, and Parsley Pie with
      hummus 173
   Hummus 146
chocolate (chocolata)
   Chocolate Pie 184
cushion, circular (kara) 35, 48
cilantro 47, 153

Chicken Pie with Cilantro and Garlic 135
cornmeal 31, 47
   Paper-Thin Bread 48
Cooked Strained Yogurt Pie 86
cracked wheat see bulgar

Dried Yogurt and Bulgar (kishk) 93, 97
   Dried Yogurt and Bulgar 97
   Kishk Pie 94
   Kishk Pie with Cheese 101
   Kishk Pie with Vegetables 102
   Kishk Pie with Walnuts 103
   Kishk Pie with Yogurt 101
   Meat Preserve Pie with Kishk 145
   Spicy Kishk Pie 98
dough ('ajeen) 42–43
   pastry dough 31, 165
   Whole-Wheat Flour and
      Bulgar Dough 63

Egg (bayd) 125
   Egg Pie 126
   Egg Pie with Cheese 129
   Egg Pie with Vegetables 129
   Armenian Sausage Pie with Eggs 181

fatayer see Turnovers
Feta Cheese Pie 83
Fresh Thyme Pie 121

garlic
   Chicken Pie with Cilantro and Garlic 135
   Hummus 146
Ground Meat, Onion, and Parsley (kafta) 167
   Ground Meat, Onion, and Parlsey Pie 169
   Ground Meat, Onion, and Parsley Pie with
      Hummus 173
   Ground Meat, Onion, and Parsley Pie with Red
      Pepper Paste 174
   Raw Meat, Onion, and Parsley Pie 170

halawa (haleweh) 32
   Halawa Pie 187
honey ('asal)
   Whey Cheese Pie with Honey 190
Hot Cheese Pie 75
Hummus 146
   Meat Preserve Pie with Hummus 146
   Ground Meat, Onion, and Parsley Pie with
      Hummus 173

kafta see Ground Meat, Onion, and Parsley
Kashkaval Cheese Pie 83
khobz see bread
kishk see Dried Yogurt and Bulgar
Kishk Pie 94
Kishk Pie with Cheese 101
Kishk Pie with Vegetables 102
Kishk Pie with Walnuts 103
Kishk Pie with Yogurt 101

labneh see strained yogurt
lamb see meat

lemon juice
   Bite-Sized Meat Pies with Strained Yogurt 162
   Chicken Pie 132
   Chicken Pie with Cilantro and Garlic 135
   Fresh Thyme Pie 121
   Hummus 146
   Purslane Turnovers 111
   Spinach Turnovers 107
   Swiss Chard Turnovers 110
   Zucchini Turnovers 108
Light Wild Thyme Pie 65

Meat (lahmeh) 32 see also Armenian Sausage,
      Chicken, Meat Preserve
   Aleppo Meat Pie 154
   Armenian Meat Pie 157
   Baalbek Bite-Sized Meat Pies 158
   Bite-Sized Meat Pies with Strained Yogurt 162
   Ground Meat, Onion, and Parsley 167
      Ground Meat, Onion, and Parsley Pie 169
      Ground Meat, Onion, and Parsley Pie with
         Hummus 173
      Ground Meat, Onion, and Parsley Pie with
         Red Pepper Paste 174
      Raw Meat, Onion, and Parsley Pie 170
   Meat Pie 151
   Meat Pie with Red Peppers 161
   Tripoli Meat Pie 165
Meat Preserve (awarma) 32, 137
   Meat Preserve Pie 138
   Meat Preserve Pie with Eggs 141
   Meat Preserve Pie with Strained Yogurt 142
   Meat Preserve Pie with Kishk 145
   Meat Preserve Pie with Hummus 146
mint 47, 54, 57, 71, 83
   Bulgari Cheese Pie 81
   Cooked Strained Yogurt Pie 86
   Egg Pie with Vegetables 129
   Ground Meat, Onion, and Parsley
      Pie (variation) 169
   Ground Meat, Onion, and Parsley Pie
      with Hummus (variation) 173
   Light Wild Thyme Pie 65
   Spiced Cheese Pie (variation) 78
   Strained Yogurt Pie 85
   Whey Cheese Pie 91
   Wild Thyme Pie with Fresh Vegetables 58
molasses (debs) 30
   Molasses and Sesame Paste Pie 189
mushroom
   Mushroom Pie 119

onion see also Ground Meat, Onion, and Parsley
   Aleppo Meat Pie 154
   Armenian Meat Pie 157
   Baalbek Bite-Sized Meat Pies 158
   Egg Pie with Vegetables 129
   Feta Cheese Pie 83
   Fresh Thyme Pie 121
   Kishk Pie with Cheese 101
   Kishk Pie with Vegetables 102
   Meat Pie 151
   Meat Pie with Red Peppers 161

Meat Preserve Pie with Kishk 145
Mushroom Pie 119
Spicy Red Pepper Pie 117
Strained Yogurt Pie 85
Vegetarian Pie 114
Wild Thyme Pie with Fresh Vegetables 58
orange blossom water (*ma'zahr*) 30
Paper-Thin Bread (*khobz marquq*) 47–48

Paper-Thin Bread (*khobz marquq*) 47–48
parsley *see also* Ground meat, Onion, and Parsley
Armenian Meat Pie 157
Bulgari Cheese Pie 81
Egg Pie with Vegetables 129
Hot Cheese Pie 75
Meat Pie with Red Peppers 161
Mushroom Pie 119
peppers *see also* red pepper paste
Armenian Meat Pie 157
Cheese Pie with Vegetables 76
Fresh Thyme Pie 121
Kishk Pie with Vegetables 102
Meat Pie with Red Peppers 161
Mushroom Pie 119
Red Pepper Paste (*ribb al-harr*) 30, 153
Spiced Cheese Pie (variation) 78
Spicy Red Pepper Pie 117
Vegetarian Pie 114
Wild Thyme Pie with Fresh Vegetables 58
pine nuts
Aleppo Meat Pie 154
Armenian Meat Pie 157
Bite-Sized Meat Pies with Strained Yogurt 162
Spicy Red Pepper Pie 117
Spinach Turnovers (variation) 107
Zucchini Turnovers (variation) 108
pomegranate syrup (*ribb al-rumman*) 30
Aleppo Meat Pie 154
Baalbek Bite-Sized Meat Pies (variation) 158
Tripoli Meat Pies 165
puff pastry
Tripoli Meat Pies 165
Purslane Turnovers 111

Ramadan Bread 197
Raw Ground Meat, Onion, and Parsley Pie 170
Red Pepper Paste (*ribb al-harr*) 30, 153
Armenian Meat Pie 157
Ground Meat, Onion, and Parsley Pie with Red
Pepper Paste 174
Hot Cheese Pie 75
Kishk Pie with Walnuts 103
Meat Pie 151
Meat Pie with Red Peppers 161
Spicy Kishk Pie 98
Spicy Red Pepper Pie 117
Whey Cheese Pie 91
Wild Thyme Pie with Red Pepper Paste 60
Wild Thyme Pie with Walnuts 63

scallions
Feta Cheese Pie 83
Whey Cheese Pie 91

sesame paste (*tahini*) 32, 154, 158, 187, 194
Hummus 146
Molasses and Sesame Paste Pie 189
Sesame Paste Bread 194
Tripoli Meat Pies 165
sesame seeds (*sumsum*) 7, 30, 32, 65
Kishk Pie 94
Kishk Pie with Cheese 101
Kishk Pie with Yogurt 101
Kishk Pie with Walnuts 103
Ramadan Bread 197
Sesame Seed Bread 193
Spicy Kishk Pie 98
Supreme Cheese Pie (variation) 72
Whey Cheese Pie 91
Wild Thyme Mixture 54
Vegetarian Pie 114
shankleesh see Spiced Cheese Balls
Spiced Cheese Balls (*shankleesh*) 32, 77
Egg Pie with Cheese 129
Spiced Cheese Pie 78
Spiced Cheese Pie with White Cheese 79
Spicy Kishk Pie 98
Spicy Red Pepper Pie 117
Spinach Turnovers 107
strained yogurt (*labneh*) 32, 85
Bite-Sized Meat Pies with Strained Yogurt 162
Cooked Strained Yogurt Pie 86
Dried Yogurt and Bulgar (*kishk*) 97
Meat Preserve Pie with Strained Yogurt 142
Strained Yogurt Pie 85
Wild Thyme Pie 57
sujuk see Armenian sausage
Supreme Cheese Pie 72
Sweet (*helou*) 183
Chocolate Pie 184
Halawa Pie 187
Molasses and Sesame Paste Pie 189
Ramadan Bread 197
Sesame Paste Bread 194
Sesame Seed Bread 193
Whey Cheese Pie with Honey 190
Swiss chard
Swiss Chard Turnovers 110

tahini *see* sesame paste
thyme *see* fresh, wild
tomato *see also* tomato paste
Armenian Meat Pie 157
Baalbek Bite-Sized Meat Pies 158
Cheese Pie with Vegetables 76
Egg Pie with Vegetables 129
Feta Cheese Pie 83
Fresh Thyme Pie 121
Hot Cheese Pie 75
Kishk Pie 94
Kishk Pie with Vegetables 102
Kishk Pie with Walnuts 103
Meat Pie 151
Meat Pie with Red Peppers 161
Meat Preserve Pie with Kishk 145
Mushroom Pie 119
Purslane Turnovers 111

Spiced Cheese Pie 78
Spiced Cheese Pie with White Cheese 79
Spicy Kishk Pie 98
Strained Yogurt Pie 85
Tomato Pie 118
Vegetarian Pie 114
Wild Thyme Pie with Fresh Vegetables 58

tomato paste 30, 75, 94, 103, 132, 161
Wild Thyme Pie with Fresh Vegetables 58
Vegetarian Pie 114
Tomato Pie 118
Tripoli Meat Pie 165
Turnovers (*fatayer*) 105
Purslane Turnovers 111
Spinach Turnovers 107
Swiss Chard Turnovers 110
Zucchini Turnovers 108

Vegetarian (*nabati*) 113 *see also* Wild Thyme,
Turnovers, bread
Chickpea Pie 122
Fresh thyme Pie 121
Mushroom Pie 119
Spicy Red Pepper Pie 117
Tomato Pie 118
Vegetarian Pie 114
Vegetarian Pie 114

Whey Cheese Pie 91
Whey Cheese Pie with Honey 190
Wild Thyme (*za'tar*) 30, 53
Aleppo thyme mixture 30, 65
Wild Thyme Mixture 30, 54
Light Wild Thyme Pie 65
Wild Thyme Pie 57
Wild Thyme Pie with Fresh Vegetables 58
Wild Thyme Pie with Red Pepper Paste 60
Wild Thyme Pie with Walnuts 65
Wild Thyme Pie with Whole-Wheat Flour
and Bulgar Dough 63
walnuts (*jawz*)
Spicy Red Pepper Pie 117
Spinach Turnovers (variation) 107
Kishk Pie with Walnuts 103
Wild Thyme Pie with Walnuts 65
Zucchini Turnovers (variation) 108

Yogurt *see also* strained yogurt, spiced cheese
balls, Dried Yogurt and Bulgar
Dried Yogurt and Bulgar (*kishk*) 31, 97
Spiced Cheese Balls (*shankleesh*) 77
strained yogurt (*labneh*) 32, 85

za'tar see wild thyme
Zucchini Turnovers 108

Thanks

شكراً

To my loving husband, Serge, who has never ceased to encourage me; to Albert, Maria, and Sarah, my children, who are the light of my life; to my mother, Laurence, from whom I inherited the love of bread-making; to my father, George, from whom I inherited a passion for photography and to both for their constant inspiration; to my sister, Gabriella, who understands very well our common journey; to Albert and Jacqueline who gave me more than they'll ever know; to Guy, Henry, Nathalie, Maurice, Caroline, Jean-Francois, Gigi, Naji, and Valerie for being my biggest fans; to Raymond Yazbeck, my faithful mentor; to the team at Ray's Photography for their encouragement and support; to Pierre Bared for always being there for me; to George and Naïm Hayek for helping me with food and photography; to Pierre Iskandar, who generously welcomed me into his restaurants with open arms; to Wadih Haddad, who introduced me to the world of French cuisine; to Nathalie Falaha, Nabih Massaad, Nadime Zablit, and Cherine Yazbeck for their contribution; to Jill Boutros and Tania Saba Mazraani, who worked for hours to make my message come out perfectly; to George Mazraani for his technical support; to Annie Kabakian for her sincere hospitality; to Coharick Ischinian for sharing her life story with me; to Fares Ishac for all the support and advice; to Chef Richard Assaf for teaching me numerous culinary skills; to Chef Riad Ismaïl for his motivating culinary talent; to Chef Elie Andraos for sharing with me his precious Lebanese recipes; to Samira Khalil and her parents for one of the most memorable days of my life; to Mounira and Antoinette Khalifeh for their patience and hospitality; to Elie-Pierre Sabbag for his support; to Bassam and Pascale Kahwaji for believing in my project; to Walid Ziadé for his devout support; to Naji and Nayla Moubarak for their friendship and good advice; to Mirna Hamady for her dedication and talent; to Edouard Cointreau for his touching gesture; to Karma Al Azmeh Valluy for her helpful tips and advice; to Wael Jamaleddine for his talent and sincere friendship. Last but not least, I am very grateful to Michel Moushabeck for taking *Man'oushé* to faraway lands. Thank you Leyla Moushabeck and the Interlink team for reviewing and perfecting the text and giving the book a great feel.